SPIKE MENDELSOHN • WITH MICHELINE MENDELSOHN

THE GOOD STUFF
COOKBOOK

PHOTOGRAPHY BY JOE SHYMANSKI

SPIKE MENDELSOHN • WITH MICHELINE MENDELSOHN

THE GOOD STUFF
COOKBOOK

PHOTOGRAPHY BY JOE SHYMANSKI

WILEY

JOHN WILEY & SONS, INC.

Library of Congress Cataloging-in-Publication Data

Mendelsohn, Spike.
The Good Stuff cookbook / Spike Mendelsohn with Micheline Mendelsohn.
p. cm.
Includes index.
ISBN 978-0-470-52792-4 (pbk.)
1. Cookery, American. 2. Cookery, International. 3. Good Stuff Eatery (Washington, D.C.) I. Mendelsohn, Micheline. II. Title.
TX715.M5365 2010
641.5973—dc22
2009026521
Printed in China
10 9 8 7 6 5 4 3 2 1

To the dynamic duo, mom and dad, who make it all possible. XO

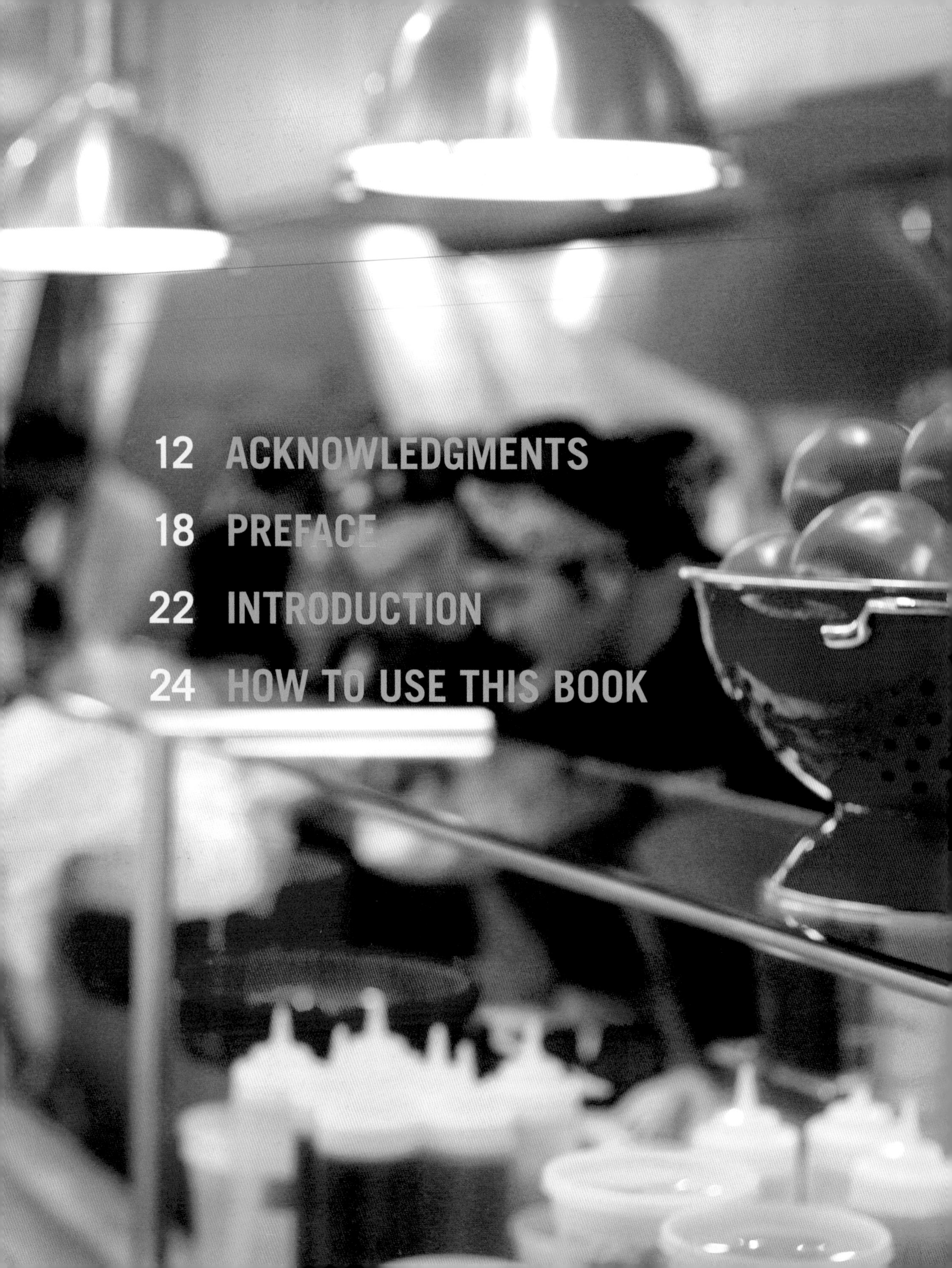

68 ERR ON THE SIDE OF . . . SIDES

116 THE GAME CHANGERS—BURGERS!

240   FAVORS 'N' FLAVORS: PARTY DISHES

252   INDEX

ACKNOWLEDGMENTS

LIFE HAS A FUNNY WAY OF REPEATING ITSELF.

When I think back to some of the experiences I've had, the people I met along the way, the ups and downs of the constantly changing restaurant world, I realize you can't ever settle or relax. Everything is always in motion—I have a lifetime ahead of me of line cooks not showing up, the paper goods order not coming in, the vegetable delivery missing crates, and the revolving door of staff—there are still a lot of memories waiting to be made.

One thing that has never changed for me is that this business, the restaurant business, is the epitome of family.

Family that grows up together, lives together, goes through ups and downs together, day in and day out. A restaurant family. It's a somewhat indescribable relationship if you've never lived it, but basically, you wake up at 6 A.M. to check in the inventory with a guy, and then bust your ass during a busy lunch and an even crazier dinner rush. You get out from cleaning around midnight and then turn to that same guy and say, "Hey man, let's go for a beer."

My parents started opening restaurants with their cousins in Montreal in 1989. After their first, they went on to open 32 restaurants across the country. They retired in 2001 and then came out of retirement to open Good Stuff Eatery in 2008 with some of those very same cousins. And like most ethnic families, our most recent project began with one telephone call that went through Greece, Florida, New York, Montreal, and Washington, D.C., faster than a car at the Indianapolis 500.

My sister, who had been living in D.C. for five years, walked past one of her neighborhood shops to find it had moved and the space was up for rent. Right then, she called my parents, who were in Greece, and convinced them to get off the beach and start calling the landlord. If you've ever been to Greece you know that this is an insane request, but my parents, being a little nuts themselves, started calling for the spot. So of course, we had to call Montreal to get some help; my mother's cousins Suzie Colivas and Peter Polatos were called simultaneously. This set in motion the big question, What type of restaurant do we open? After we settled that, I got a call about menu planning. I told Mike Colletti, my partner in crime at Mai House in NYC, that we needed help with a burger menu. The final piece was convincing my longtime friend

"DAD—THANKS FOR ALWAYS THROWING ME OUT OF THE OFFICE."

Nic Georgeades to move from Florida to D.C. to launch the restaurant.

We all lived on twin beds and couches at my parent's house for the first six weeks. No joke. During that time, I had also convinced Brian Lacayo of New York City to move to D.C. My mother was cooking for all of us, but then again, it never really mattered how many people were at my mom's house; she always cooked for an army. And this is how we came to launch Good Stuff Eatery.

So there's no particular order these thanks are in—it's the existence of these people, this family, that has come together to push me, to keep me grounded, to allow me all the opportunities that I hope continue to come my way, that I can't thank enough.

Mike Colletti, for sharing the same vision on what this business is all about and making that commitment to move to D.C. and begin the restaurant group with us because, in case you didn't realize it, you signed up for life. Also, for your dedication, opinions, and support in helping me test out all these recipes!

Nic Georgeades, for helping me peel 100 pounds of shrimp back in the day at Pepin's and for helping me peel 100 pounds of potatoes now at Good Stuff. We've both had ups and downs but it's nice to see you when I walk into the store, even if you're slacking out back on the phone.

Brian Lacayo, for saving me from all the line cooks who wanted to kick my ass! You're a pro on the grill, on the floor, in the office, and it's awesome to have you as part of the team.

Jon Malysiak, my literary agent, for seeing me on the show and getting on a plane from Chicago to D.C. to convince us this was possible. We made it! Your guidance along the way was invaluable, and you've been phenomenal to work with.

Alexandra Greeley, I still apologize for being an hour late to our interview (I would not recommend this with a food writer), but thanks for waiting and in the meantime talking with my sister, who asked you to help in the editing process. Your recommendations and editing skills were a welcome relief and absolutely necessary to finish on deadline!

Justin Schwartz and the whole team at Wiley, for believing in me and the Good Stuff philosophy and working to make this book happen. I'm so grateful for all the hours you've put in!

Billy Ivey and Ted McCoig, the "Branding Geniuses", because they brought Good Stuff Eatery to life for us and gave our cow his heart.

Bess Pappas, our designer, for her love, caring, and patience through the million changes along the way. Most of all for her outstanding design.

Vince McCoullough, our architect, contractor, assistant designer, consultant, shrink, taster . . . who invested his heart in us.

Richard Patterson, our dear friend who showed a rare intuition and the confidence in us when we needed it.

Joe Shymanski, because what started out as a meeting at Eastern Market on Capitol Hill in Washington between my sister and this incredibly talented photographer has turned into the position I've dubbed "family photographer for life." From shooting pre-construction to me in NYC, to opening night and many more events, you are truly amazing, and I'm glad you came on for this project.

To my entire family for their help and support—I'm Greek so I have about 65 cousins; couldn't include everyone but here are a few of the key players along the way . . . .

Suzie Colivas, for getting it all started and making sure we chose the tomato red instead of the plum red color for the awning and mushroom beige instead of smoky beige for the wall paint. For sacrificing your time, interrupting your life, and for the laughs we shared to make this all possible.

Peter Polatos, our partner and cousin, for believing in the concept and our abilities to make it work and grow the vision. I hope Andrew and Michael enjoy it as much as I do and we can eventually pull them in to make fourth generation restaurateurs. Pete—I promise I'll get around to naming a burger after you!

Alyssa Shelasky, for not putting me in the bachelor issue! Most importantly, for taking my ups and downs, accepting me for who I am, and making me a better man . . . I love you, Lys.

Auntie Dorothy, for showing us that your zest for life should never end, who told my dad when he sold his restaurant at 60 years old that he needed to find a job right away to keep busy and make a living. You are really Good Stuff!

Zas, my grandmother and the matriarch of the family. For teaching us what staying together and looking out for each other really

"ON A PERSONAL NOTE TO MY BROTHER SPIKE, I WANT TO THANK YOU FOR DEVOTING YOURSELF AND YOUR TALENTS TO GOOD STUFF AND MAKING THE DREAM WAY MORE THAN A RESTAURANT. YOUR MOVING TO D.C. FROM NYC COMPLETED THE FAMILY CIRCLE, AND BEING ABLE TO SPEND MOST OF OUR DAYS TOGETHER IS REALLY THE BEST STUFF." —*MICHELINE*

means. For doing everything with such grace and a smile and always being excited to hear from me.

To our Papou. My mother once wrote me that "A legacy means that you mattered, that you are remembered, that your warmth and love like an heirloom have been passed on. It will tell the future generation of our family what defines them!" I can honestly say that not a day goes by that I don't remember my grandfather's warmth and love towards life. Good Stuff to my grandfather was not a restaurant or a cookbook; it was a way of life, and I can only hope that one day my sister and I can pass on the Good Stuff family legacy on to our children and the people we meet along life's journey.

Mom, without you I wouldn't even know what the word *family* means. Thanks for always pulling us together, especially now, for this restaurant group and coming out of retirement to give Mich and me a way to make a living for us and our families. And for allowing me to pursue a path alongside that of the restaurant and believing in my skills—and just for being my biggest fan. I hope I made it as your good Greek son who still wants his bar mitzvah money back.

Dad, thanks for always throwing me out of the office! Every time you came upstairs, it seemed like there was always something: The busboy didn't clean the table, the trash was too full, the line needed someone else . . . but all of those were lessons in being a restaurant owner—you thought I wasn't paying attention but I was. And thanks for the money talks, the lease talks, for all the business sense you took time to teach me. Most of all for being a loving father and such a loving husband. Don't forget, I'm the number one world's best GM.

Cliff, my brother-in-law, for his constant support and help, and for making my sister so happy. Most of all for jumping on the line those first few weeks when the insanity began! We've sucked you into the restaurant and I am so happy you're along for this ride.

Mich, my sister, my confidante, my partner in crime. To say "I could never have done this book without you" is like calling the sky blue. As everybody knows, I've never been able to do anything meaningful without my sister. Looking back at pictures from our childhood lemonade stands, I drift back in time, with me rocking the boom box and you rocking all the important stuff. Even then, you held my hand,

you had my back, you let me be me. You've been the single most loyal and loving person in my life, whether I was a confused teenager or *Top Chef* wannabe (and *yes*, you get full credit for getting me on the show). I mean, you even found the location for Good Stuff Eatery! You've made so many of my dreams come true. Thank you, Michy. And now you're a mother and me, an uncle. So, on this book, our latest bro/sis collaboration, I swear to give your daughter all the unconditional love, support, patience, protection, comfort, and encouragement you've given me. Not to mention, she's also getting my Greek name. Calm down, people, she won't be called Spike, it's Evangelina, as in Evangelos. The fact that it's a middle name and she's really named after our mother, Catherine, is beside the point. One last thing, since I'm predictably past deadline—and inevitably driving my beloved big sister up the wall . . . just remember . . . love ya.

To the casting crew at Magical Elves and Bravo who put me in the fourth season of *Top Chef: Chicago*, one of the most exhausting, grueling, and best experiences I've ever had. Particularly to Andy Cohen and Victoria (Tory) Brody and their team, who continue to support me along the way and have become part of the family.

A cookbook can't be written without giving thanks to the training in the kitchen, on the floor, and during those late night drinks when you're exhausted from service. To the greats who have helped me along the way:

Drew Nieporent and Myriad Restaurant Group; Michael Huynh of Mai House; Gérard Boyer and Les Crayères; Thomas Keller and Bouchon; the Maccioni family of Le Cirque.

Art Smith, whose success and accomplishments in the kitchen and constant generosity towards humanity are inspiring for any young chef. His warm personality is infectious and he's become family.

José Andrés, who gave me the best opening night gift for Good Stuff Eatery. Chef came in and took the time to see what we were doing and gave advice on how we could make our restaurant better for our staff and our customers—we loved it. Learning from a master is the best way. I hope that as my family opens more places, he'll continue to do that.

THANK YOU.

GOOOOOD
STUUUUUFFF!

So, in order to enjoy my guilty indulgence and make everyone enjoy theirs, my family and I opened Good Stuff Eatery, a restaurant that focuses on farm-fresh ingredients right from the farm to your table.

How do I make this more challenging? Go into business with my parents, make my sister quit her job to do public relations, move my three closest friends to D.C., smuggle a cousin from Canada, and install a restaurant in what used to be a paper store and a bank.

But Good Stuff isn't just a burger place, it's a lifestyle, and the menu reflects that. We've thought out every single thing. We turn our own custard to make our hand-spun milkshakes; we researched many meat blends and picked the best; we use a potato for fries that no other restaurant uses but can be found at your grocery store. None of this is just to be different, it's simply to be delicious.

What is close to us, as you will see, is our menu and this cookbook, which reflect our families' and friends' experiences and favorite memories. What I mean is that everything on the menu has meaning to us. The name, Good Stuff Eatery, comes from my grandfather, Sunny Nakis. Whenever he enjoyed something in life he always gave a fist pump in the air (like those hockey players he grew up with) and said "Goooood, Stuuuuufff!"

"EVERYTHING HAS A MEANING TO US."

What makes this restaurant unique is the constant striving for perfection for the good stuff. Not a day goes by that my mother doesn't tell me the fries are salted too much, or that they are not hot enough. Not a day goes by that Mike doesn't taste the custard to make sure its consistency and flavor is spot-on. Not a day goes by that Nic isn't reworking operations of the restaurant for better service. Not a day goes by that Brian isn't calling a supplier because he thinks the product can be better or that my father isn't running around making sure he's keeping us all on our toes. What I'm saying is if a family shows this much love to a hamburger, you're going to have a great time.

I'm going to bring in a little ego here for a sec: I trained in France, Vietnam, worked at some of the best places in the world, with some of the greats—Keller, Huynh, Nieporent, Maccioni, Boyer. Why a hamburger joint?

Because this style of restaurant embodies my philosophy: Give people simple, delicious, fresh American comfort food using local, fresh, farm-grown ingredients. We take old favorites and make them new, different, and hip, giving them the "good stuff twist."

You know, "Good Stuff" is more than a descriptive title. It's a declaration, an inspiration, and a rallying cry. Because Good Stuff Eatery isn't just another burger joint. We're on a mission to bring together good food, good times, good people, and good-ness in a place where good stuff means more than just better-than-average food. We believe that good stuff should be a way of life. Eat up!

After three generations making food our life's work and passion, we offer Americans their favorite foods made with delicious farm-fresh ingredients, respecting our environment and sourcing our products from our local farming community.

These recipes won't take you all day to create. In fact, I hope you will prepare these delicious meals with family and friends, making your own very special memories.

So turn on the Beatles, throw on some cheeseburgers, and top them with some ruby red tomatoes and a lovin' spoonful of Good Stuff Sauce. Make a batch of Sunny's Fries and Sriracha Mayo for dipping, spin some Toasted Marshmallow Milkshakes, and bring out the brownies you made on Sunday.

NOW YOU JUST MADE THE GOOD STUFF!

If you just bought this book, consider yourself privileged to have come upon it, because you have now become part of the inner circle I call the Good Stuffers. Together, we are the voice of reason when it comes to the infamous hamburger, hand-spun shakes, and fries. You are now part of the movement that loves good food, good times, and good people.

My family, friends, and I have a mutual love we share with the rest of the world when it comes to comfort foods. When we first started conceptualizing Good Stuff Eatery in Washington, D.C., we all agreed that if we were going to take on America's favorite comfort foods, we would have no choice but to take them to the next level. After countless hours of cooking and tasting burgers, fries, wedge salads, shakes, and more, we finally had our epiphany: The secret to good food is a lot of things, but most importantly it is the people you choose to share it with. So make sure you are in Good Stuff Company!

The second best secret is your grocery list. Always shop for the freshest and in-season ingredients. When it comes to your meat blend, develop a good relationship with your local butcher. This way, you can specify exactly what you would like, and he can have it ground freshly for you. If you're lucky, he might even have a couple tips for you—after all, he is a butcher! After you get your meat, the next thing you need to figure out is how you're going to cook it. Most people fire up the grill in the backyard, and I'm all for that method; there is nothing better than cooking outside. I also love the char-grilled flavor that develops when grilling, so don't forget your charcoal and grilling tools, and maybe a cute apron if you're into that kind of thing. I know my father is! At Good Stuff Eatery, we use a flat top grill because we love the way it sears the hamburger, developing great flavor and texture. Instead of all the juices dripping and marinating the charcoal, they marinate the burger. You can achieve this by pan-searing in a sauté pan or skillet in your kitchen or buying a plancha to put on your grill. Both techniques are great. Just make sure you have fun. One thing I do not recommend is poaching your burger.

In addition to love, blend of meat, and cooking technique, there are a few more things that distinguish my burgers from everyday burgers.

INTRODUCTION

I do whatever it takes to infuse maximum flavor into each of the components that make my hamburgers what they are—I use good sauces and toppings, cooking techniques, and seasoning. When you use this book, you will see that I pride myself on flavorful and balanced sauces, and tasty and textured toppings like our Colletti Smokehouse—the spicy, sweet, sour BBQ sauce with fried Vidalia onion rings that give it a great crunch. It wins them over every time! As far as technique goes, I love searing my burgers (which tightens up the meat), so make sure you rest the hamburger before assembling. This way, the juices redistribute through the burger, leaving you with a perfectly cooked juicy burger. Working on your temperature also comes with experience. I personally like medium rare.

Let's not forget about seasoning. This skill also comes with experience, but don't be afraid of the S/P. That's what I call salt and pepper. Use it. It makes a world of difference, and I promise you by the end of this book, you will be a pro!

The only thing that can make a burger better at this point is what you serve it with. I'm talking about the side dishes, fries, and milkshakes. There are a million sides out there, so I won't get into that right now. At Good Stuff Eatery, we are as equally proud of our shakes and fries as we are of our burgers. We make fresh custard every day, and that is what we make our shakes with. Throw some creative flavorings and toppings in the mix, and you have the best shakes in the world.

Okay, so how do you make custard at home? Well, that's simple . . . you don't. Ice cream will work great too, but if you look hard enough at the grocery store, you will probably find frozen custard. I like it because it's thicker and creamier. And make sure you have a blender on hand, because you do not want to be whisking away on a Sunday afternoon.

This leads us to french fries. Now, it would be too easy if I told you what type of potato I use (and my mother would kill me), so here is some good direction. Who says you have to use an Idaho potato to make the best french fry? Who says you have to leave the peel on or not? My advice is, go to the store and buy a variety—red, yellow, and even purple potatoes—and just have fun. I will say, though, that aging your potatoes is a good trick. (Yes, I said aging your potatoes!) This means storing your potatoes for up to six months in a temperature-controlled cool environment. Aging allows the starches to convert into sugars, giving you a sweeter potato. I also recommend blanching your potatoes before frying. This means frying them once at a lower temperature, around 250°F, and then letting them cool before frying them a second time to a golden crisp at 350°F. Make sure you salt them right out of the oil so the seasoning sticks! Of course, you will need frying equipment—a large sauce pot or stock pot will do, along with a frying basket. Or, make it easy on yourself and get a fryolater. Make sure to only fill it with oil three-quarters of the way up, because the oil will rise when frying. As far as the oil goes, peanut oil has a higher smoking point, which will fry your potatoes crispier, and canola oil is a great neutral oil. If you're really feeling it, lard is by far the best way to go!

HOW TO USE THIS BOOK

OUR SECRET

Don't overthink! There are just five building blocks that make up a Spike burger. Grab a pencil: It's the meat, buns, toppings, cheese, and finishing touches. That's it. However, it's precisely because hamburgers are so simple and have so few components that it's vital you use the best-quality ingredients. If the quality of any of the building blocks is substandard, the burger will be okay but never outstanding. In this cookbook, I address all five of these components, giving you professional and *unprofessional* tips and kitchen smarts.

THE PARTY PLAN

Because I love burgers so much, I often make a party of it, choosing a menu of three to four burgers, a couple of shakes, sides, and sweets. The potential menu variations are endless. If you're playing host(ess), it's always a little easier to go "slider" style, with mini shakes and some family-style shared side dishes. Traditionally, sliders should be a little over 2 ounces of meat. Adjust the patty sizes accordingly. Then, either buy slider buns *or* take a 3-inch ring mold (which is essentially a cookie cutter) and cut out slider buns from regular buns. Follow the recipes and techniques as written, but adjust the cooking times. Sliders are major crowd-pleasers, I promise.

PERSONALLY SPEAKING

When planning a party, the single best advice I can give you is to plan appropriately and prep as much as you can in advance. It takes the pressure off and makes it almost impossible to get caught in any kind of dinner party disaster! Also, remember to taste everything. Taste your combinations of flavors. Taste the before and after versions when you're seasoning. Also, take risks! You want to mix and match toppings and cheeses. In fact, if you stumble across a real winner, e-mail us at info@goodstuffeatery.com, and maybe we'll put it on the menu (and name it after you!).

DON'T OVER-THINK!

LISTS

Chefs are a little disorganized by nature. We specialize in the other side of the brain thinking, you know? So, most of us live by our lists—to-do lists, grocery lists, notes to self, etc. Here are a few lists from me to you. Basically, if you want to make these recipes and turn a new corner in the kitchen, the following should be your burger bible.

YOUR PANTRY LIST

ONE. Olive oil—okay, I'm really not sure why you need this, but I'm Greek, and olive oil is my first rule of life.

TWO. Mayonnaise—you can make it from scratch, but Hellmann's double egg is fantastic!

THREE. Sriracha—a versatile Thai chili sauce for those who like things hot.

FOUR. Condensed milk—this always comes in handy when you want to incorporate sweet tones into your food.

FIVE. Marshmallows—gotta have 'em to make the most popular item in the book, the Toasted Marshmallow Shake.

SIX. Salt—keep kosher salt for regular seasoning, but stock a couple of fancy finishing salts for that extra little touch, especially when it comes to your sides and fries.

SEVEN. Molasses—you may see it come up in a recipe or two. It's such a unique flavor and fun to play with, but it is a sticky mess, so stay focused!

EIGHT. Rice wine vinegar—use it just like regular vinegar. It has a naturally sweet tone and really delicious flavor.

NINE. Assorted chips—they make for a quick substitution if you can't get around to French fries.

TEN. Pepper mill—I know this not an ingredient, but fresh cracked pepper truly makes a difference on your wedges (salads), fries, and maybe even shakes if you're into that kind of thing. Don't forget to stock black peppercorns, but the pink ones can come in handy too.

YOUR FRIDGE LIST

ONE. Herbs—stock all sorts: mint, tarragon, cilantro, Thai basil, thyme, marjoram, and oregano.

TWO. Applewood-smoked bacon—my personal favorite. I like the smoky tones, but bacon is bacon, so buy any kind, even turkey bacon. P.S. Do you know I sign all my letters "Love & Bacon, Spike!"?

THREE. Cheese—hello, we are making burgers here, so the classic fave is square yellow American, but stock up with all sorts of cheese and just have a melty old time with it.

FOUR. Beer.

FIVE. Butter—salted, unsalted, just make sure it's there.

SIX. Pickles—salty ones, sweet ones, sour ones. Pickles always complement food because they really cleanse your palate and accentuate your taste buds.

SEVEN. Nice ripe tomatoes—and please take these out of the fridge, because cold temperature stunts the ripening process. Do the tomato justice and put it by the window to ripen up.

EIGHT. Potatoes—yellow ones, Idaho, Red Bliss, even purple ones!

NINE. Onions—Vidalias (the sweet ones), red onions, Spanish onions—you will be using all of these throughout the cookbook.

TEN. Chocolate—it's an aphrodisiac and a great thing to nibble on when you're cooking. It might even make you more creative, but don't spoil your appetite!!

MUST-HAVE TOOLS
FOR THE KITCHEN

- Grill (and charcoal)
- Deep fryer
- Blender
- Microplane graters
- Spice grinder
- Brush (and a grill brush)
- BBQ tools
- Nonstick pans
- Peeler
- A good chef's knife and a paring knife
- Cast-iron pans

Did I forget anything? Probably. Well, the best part about being a chef is the freedom to improvise. Don't take yourself too seriously in the kitchen, have fun, try to plan ahead, taste everything, and turn up the music.

THE GOOD STUFF
IS STARTING ...
NOW

CONDIMENTS & COMPLEMENTS—MAYONNAISES & SAUCES

1

HOMEMADE BASIC MAYONNAISE

GOOD STUFF SAUCE

CHIPOTLE MAYONNAISE

CHIPOTLE PESTO

SRIRACHA MAYONNAISE

OLD BAY MAYONNAISE

MANGO MAYONNAISE

BALSAMIC MAYONNAISE

CURRY MAYONNAISE

POMEGRANATE MAYONNAISE

MUSTARD SEED MAYONNAISE

MAYOLIVE

We were living in **Seville**, Spain, because my parents owned and operated twelve restaurants at the World Exposition in Seville in **1992**. I was a lanky 11-year-old working at the American Pavilion, running around and getting all the visiting celebrities whatever they needed. My scrawniness made it easy to get around. My memory of growing up during that time was being overworked and underpaid and loving every single minute of it. During that time my parents took my sister and me all over Europe; we traveled every chance we got. One of our side trips was to **Amsterdam**. It hits you—fries in **mayo**—I mean, are you serious? Is there anything better than this? It's part of me, I can't help it, and I can never eat fries without mayo.

HOMEMADE
BASIC MAYONNAISE (MAKES ABOUT 2 CUPS)

In France, they used to make fun of me about my love of Hellmann's, but if you ask me, it's pretty damn good. If you want to go the extra mile, though, it doesn't get any more basic than this recipe.

- 2 large eggs
- 4 teaspoons Dijon mustard
- 2 teaspoons white wine vinegar
- 1 teaspoon sea salt
- 2 cups grapeseed oil

Add the eggs, mustard, vinegar, and salt to a food processor or blender. Process for 30 seconds in the food processor, or for 10 seconds in the blender. With the motor running, drizzle in the oil slowly at first, then add in a thin, steady stream until all the oil is added and the mixture is smooth. Stop the motor and taste. If the sauce is too thick, thin it with a little hot water. If too thin, process a little longer. The mayonnaise can be refrigerated in an airtight container for up to 1 week.

GOOD STUFF
SAUCE (MAKES ABOUT 2 CUPS)

After reading several books and articles on Americans and the hamburgers they love, my mother found that people's favorite sauces were different takes on Thousand Island dressing (ketchup and mayo). At one of our family tastings, Mike Colletti, a chef I met at Le Cirque, and I came up with our twist on it—we locked ourselves in the kitchen and added a little something to the sauce to give it a real kick.

2 cups Homemade Basic
   Mayonnaise (page 34)
2 tablespoons ketchup

2 tablespoons molasses
2 tablespoons rice vinegar
1 teaspoon salt

Add the mayonnaise, ketchup, molasses, vinegar, and salt to a food processor or blender. Puree until smooth. The sauce can be refrigerated in an airtight container for up to 1 week.

CHIPOTLE
MAYONNAISE (MAKES ABOUT 3 CUPS)

Chipotle chiles are dried and smoked jalapeños, readily available canned in a thick pickling sauce (adobo).

2 cups Homemade Basic Mayonnaise (page 34)

1 cup Chipotle Pesto (page 37)

2 tablespoons sweetened condensed milk

1 tablespoon salt

Add the mayonnaise, Chipotle Pesto, condensed milk, and salt to a food processor or blender. Puree until smooth. The mayonnaise can be refrigerated in an airtight container for up to 1 week.

CHIPOTLE
PESTO (MAKES ABOUT 2½ CUPS)

1 7-ounce can chipotles in adobo
1 cup fresh cilantro leaves
½ cup fresh lime juice
½ cup fresh basil leaves

½ red onion, coarsely chopped
4 cloves garlic
3 sun-dried tomatoes
1 teaspoon sea salt

½ teaspoon freshly ground black pepper
½ cup extra virgin olive oil

Add the chipotles, cilantro, lime juice, basil, onion, garlic, sun-dried tomatoes, salt, and pepper to a food processor. Pulse to mix well. With the motor running, drizzle in the oil slowly at first, then add in a thin, steady stream until all the oil is added and the mixture is smooth. Strain through a fine-mesh strainer. Taste and adjust the seasonings, if needed. The pesto can be refrigerated in an airtight container for up to 1 week.

SRIRACHA
MAYONNAISE (MAKES ABOUT 2½ CUPS)

A chile-fired sauce from Thailand, sriracha consists primarily of ground red chiles and vinegar. Traditionally used for seasoning seafood dishes, sriracha also adds a kick to soups, curries, and stews and has become a popular condiment in the United States. It is readily available in Asian markets and many well-stocked supermarkets.

2 cups Homemade Basic
   Mayonnaise (page 34)
½ cup sriracha hot sauce

2 tablespoons sweetened
   condensed milk

Add the mayonnaise, sriracha, and condensed milk to a food processor or blender. Puree until smooth. The mayonnaise can be refrigerated in an airtight container for up to 1 week.

OLD BAY
MAYONNAISE (MAKES ABOUT 2 CUPS)

When in Rome . . . did we think we'd get away from making an Old Bay Mayo so close to the Crab Capital of the World? Maryland is literally 10 minutes away! We couldn't resist.

2 cups Homemade Basic
  Mayonnaise (page 34)
½ cup Old Bay seasoning
2 tablespoons light brown
  sugar

Grated zest and juice
  from 1 lemon

Add the mayonnaise, seasoning, brown sugar, and lemon zest and juice to a food processor or blender. Puree until smooth. The mayonnaise can be refrigerated in an airtight container for up to 1 week.

MANGO
MAYONNAISE (MAKES ABOUT 3 CUPS)

1 cup store-bought Major
   Grey's Mango Chutney
2 cups Homemade Basic
   Mayonnaise (page 34)

2 tablespoons sweetened
   condensed milk

Add the mango chutney to a food processor. Puree until smooth. Add the mayonnaise and condensed milk. Puree until smooth. The mayonnaise can be refrigerated in an airtight container for up to 1 week.

BALSAMIC
MAYONNAISE (MAKES ABOUT 3 CUPS)

1 cup balsamic vinegar
   plus a splash
¼ cup sugar
   Grated zest from ½
   orange

2 cups Homemade Basic
   Mayonnaise (page 34)

Combine 1 cup of the vinegar, the sugar, and orange zest in a large saucepan over medium heat. Cook, stirring constantly, until the mixture thickens and becomes syrupy.

Add the mixture and the mayonnaise to a food processor or blender. Puree until smooth. Stir in the splash of vinegar to bring out the vinegar taste. The mayonnaise can be refrigerated in an airtight container for up to 1 week.

CURRY
MAYONNAISE (MAKES ABOUT 4 CUPS)

1 cup curry powder
2 cups Homemade Basic
    Mayonnaise (page 34)
1 cup sweetened
    condensed milk

½ cup golden raisins
  Salt

Sprinkle the curry powder into a dry skillet and heat over low heat. Toast, stirring constantly to prevent burning, until fragrant, about 1 minute. In a bowl, stir together the curry powder, mayonnaise, and condensed milk until combined. Fold in the raisins and add salt to taste. The mayonnaise can be refrigerated in an airtight container for up to 1 week.

POMEGRANATE
MAYONNAISE (MAKES ABOUT 3 CUPS)

In season during fall and winter months, the pomegranate is filled with ruby red seeds that are cherished for their tart-sweet flavor and health benefits. The seeds are easy to extract, but some well-stocked supermarkets carry fresh pomegranate seeds packed in plastic bags. Look for pomegranate molasses in Middle Eastern markets or buy it from online suppliers.

2 cups Homemade Basic
   Mayonnaise (page 34)
½ cup pomegranate
   molasses

1 tablespoon red wine
   vinegar
½ cup pomegranate seeds

In a bowl, stir together the mayonnaise, molasses, and vinegar until well combined. Fold in the pomegranate seeds. The mayonnaise can be refrigerated in an airtight container for up to 1 week.

MUSTARD
SEED MAYONNAISE (MAKES ABOUT 3 CUPS)

2 cups Homemade Basic
  Mayonnaise (page 34)
1 cup whole-grain mustard
1 tablespoon Dijon
  mustard

1 tablespoon sherry
  vinegar
1 tablespoon light brown
  sugar

Add the mayonnaise, mustards, vinegar, and brown sugar to a food processor or blender. Puree until smooth. The mayonnaise can be refrigerated in an airtight container for up to 1 week.

MAYOLIVE (MAKES ABOUT 3 CUPS)

This is a true recipe of my favorite things to dip French fries into—mayonnaise and tapenade. The Mediterranean influence comes from putting tapenade on everything I eat and of course, you can't go wrong with mayo! The flavors are amazing.

A robustly flavored paste based on capers, olives, and lemon juice, tapenade is readily available commercially in most supermarkets and specialty food stores.

2 cups Homemade Basic Mayonnaise (page 34)
1 cup store-bought tapenade
2 tablespoons red wine vinegar
2 tablespoons minced red onion
Anchovy fillets, optional
Freshly ground black pepper

Add the mayonnaise, tapenade, vinegar, and onion to a food processor or blender. Add the anchovies to taste, if using, and pepper to taste. Puree until smooth. The mayonnaise can be refrigerated in an airtight container for up to 1 week.

WEDGE WITH AN EDGE: SALADS

2

The **wedge** salad hasn't had it easy. First it was hot, then it was not. Some say too basic, too **crunchy**, too retro, but for all those reasons, I'm committed to bringing the wedge back! Of course, not all wedges are created equal. As you'll see, I take classic salad favorites and wedge 'em out, resulting in a heartier, crispier, **sexier** salad. Mesclun, what?

FARM-FRESH
GREEK WEDGE (SERVES 4)

My family grew up on *horiatiki*, or Greek salad. It's a country salad of juicy tomatoes, crisp cucumbers, sliced red onions, crumbly feta cheese, and plump kalamata olives. We make this at almost every meal, and when we're in Greece, and the vegetables are at their very best, it's the most delicious thing I've ever tasted. We tweaked it a bit for our special wedge menu at the restaurant and added the toasted sesame seeds (they make all the difference).

CHAMPAGNE VINAIGRETTE
- ¼ cup Champagne vinegar
- 2 tablespoons Dijon mustard
- 2 teaspoons honey
- ¾ teaspoon sea salt
- ¼ teaspoon freshly ground black pepper
- ¼ cup extra virgin olive oil

SALAD
- 4 teaspoons sesame seeds
- 1 head iceberg lettuce
- ½ pound mixed greens
- 1 seedless cucumber, cut in half lengthwise and thinly sliced
- 1 cup pitted kalamata olives
- 4 ounces grape tomatoes, cut in half
- 8 ounces feta cheese, crumbled
- 4 teaspoons snipped fresh dill
- 2 scallions, sliced
- 1 red onion, cut in half and sliced
- Sea salt and freshly ground black pepper

To make the dressing, add the vinegar, mustard, honey, salt, and pepper to a food processor or blender and blend to combine. With the motor running, drizzle in the oil slowly at first, then add in a thin, steady stream until all the oil is added. Refrigerate until ready to use.

To make the salad, preheat the oven to 350°F. Spread out the sesame seeds on a baking sheet in a single layer. Toast for about 5 minutes, or until light brown. Remove and cool.

Remove the root end from the lettuce and cut the head into 4 wedges. Place one wedge each on four individual serving dishes. Scatter the mixed greens around each wedge. Top each wedge with cucumber, olives, tomatoes, and feta. Garnish each portion with the dill, toasted sesame seeds, scallions, and onion. Dress each wedge with 2 tablespoons of the dressing and season with salt and pepper.

FARM-FRESH
CAESAR WEDGE (SERVES 4)

I've never met a foodie who didn't have a Caesar salad fetish. They're simple yet snobby, easy yet impressive, healthy yet . . . not. Personally I could call Caesar salad a meal, but sometimes it's also a sensational starter.

CAESAR DRESSING
- 2 large egg yolks
- 3 garlic cloves
- 4 tablespoons white wine vinegar
- ½ teaspoon sea salt
- ½ teaspoon Worcestershire sauce
- ½ teaspoon Dijon mustard
- ¼ teaspoon freshly ground black pepper
- 2 salt-packed anchovy fillets
- ½ cup extra virgin olive oil
- 2 tablespoons freshly grated Parmesan cheese

CROUTONS
- 4 potato rolls
- 2 tablespoons extra virgin olive oil
- 2 garlic cloves, minced
- 1 tablespoon garlic salt
- 1 tablespoon freshly grated Parmesan cheese
- 1½ teaspoons dried oregano
- 1 teaspoon freshly ground black pepper

SALAD
- 1 pound applewood-smoked bacon
- 1 head iceberg lettuce
- ½ pound mixed greens
  Sea salt and freshly ground black pepper
- 1 cup freshly grated Parmesan cheese

To make the dressing, add the yolks, garlic, vinegar, salt, Worcestershire, mustard, pepper, and anchovies to a food processor or blender and blend to combine. With the motor running, drizzle in the oil slowly at first, then add in a thin, steady stream until all the oil is added. Once thick, add the Parmesan and pulse once. Refrigerate until ready to use.

To make the croutons, preheat the oven to 350°F. Cut the rolls into ¼-inch-thick cubes. In a mixing bowl, combine the cubes with the oil, garlic, garlic salt, Parmesan, oregano, and pepper and toss. Spread on a baking sheet. Bake for 10 to 15 minutes, or until golden brown.

To make the salad, heat a skillet over medium heat and cook the bacon until crisp. Line a metal tray with paper towels. Drain the bacon. Cool, crumble, and set aside.

Remove the root end from the lettuce and cut the head into 4 wedges. Place one wedge each on four individual serving dishes. Scatter the mixed greens around each wedge. Dress each wedge with 2 tablespoons of dressing and season with the salt and pepper. Garnish each with the crumbled bacon, Parmesan, and croutons.

FARM-FRESH
ENSALADA WEDGE (SERVES 4)

The majority of my adolescence was spent at my family's restaurant, Pepin's, in St. Petersburg, Florida. This wedge emulates our signature salad, a mixture of manzanilla olives, fresh tomatoes, and cottonseed vinaigrette. I made this bad boy for years . . . why stop now?

RED WINE VINAIGRETTE
- ½ cup red wine vinegar
- ½ red onion, chopped
- 2 tablespoons Dijon mustard
- 2 tablespoons honey
- 1 garlic clove, minced
- 1 teaspoon dried oregano
- ½ teaspoon sea salt
- ½ teaspoon freshly ground black pepper
- 1 cup vegetable oil

SALAD
- 1 head iceberg lettuce
- ½ pound mixed greens
- 1½ cups pitted manzanilla olives
- 1 pint grape tomatoes, cut in half
- 1 cup thinly sliced scallions
- 1 cup thinly sliced red onion
- 1 cup freshly grated Parmesan cheese
- 2 cups Roasted Corn and Red Pepper Salsa (page 104)
- 2 cups crushed corn tortilla chips

To make the dressing, add the vinegar, onion, mustard, honey, garlic, oregano, salt, and pepper to a food processor or blender and blend to combine. With the motor running, drizzle in the oil slowly at first, then add in a thin, steady stream until all the oil is added and the mixture is smooth. Set aside until ready to use.

To make the salad, remove the root end from the lettuce, and cut the head into 4 wedges. Place one wedge each on four individual serving dishes. Scatter the mixed greens around each wedge. Dress each wedge with 2 tablespoons of the dressing. Top with the olives, tomatoes, scallions, and onion and sprinkle each salad with Parmesan. Top each with ½ cup of the Red Pepper and Corn Salsa and garnish each with tortilla chips.

FARM-FRESH
CLASSIC WEDGE (SERVES 4)

We use the word *classic* quite literally here. This is the ultimate wedge salad. The wedge's wedge, if you will! The marriage of blue cheese crumble and crispy, crunchy iceberg is simply genius. Naturally, we had to take it to another level with fried Vidalia onion petals. Yup, you're welcome.

BLUE CHEESE DRESSING
- 1 cup buttermilk
- 1 cup sour cream
- 4 ounces blue cheese, crumbled
- 6 tablespoons white wine vinegar
- 1 teaspoon honey
- 1 teaspoon sea salt
- 1 teaspoon freshly ground black pepper

SALAD
- 1 pound applewood-smoked bacon
- 1 head iceberg lettuce
- ½ pound mixed greens
- 8 ounces blue cheese, crumbled
- 2 cups thinly sliced red onion
- 1 cup thinly sliced scallions

- 2 cups Cliff's Homegrown Vidalia Onion Petals (page 81), optional

To make the dressing, add all the ingredients to a blender or food processor and blend to combine. Set aside until ready to use.

To make the salad, heat a skillet over medium heat and cook the bacon until crisp. Line a metal tray with paper towels. Drain the bacon. Cool, crumble, and set aside.

Remove the root end from the lettuce, and cut the head into 4 wedges. Place one wedge each on four individual serving dishes. Scatter the mixed greens around each wedge. Dress each wedge with 2 tablespoons of the dressing. Garnish each with the crumbled bacon, cheese, onion, and scallions. Top each with ½ cup of Cliff's Homegrown Vidalia Onion Petals, if using.

FRIED GOAT CHEESE, DRIED CRANBERRIES, AND ALMOND WEDGE (SERVES 4)

Some salads are show-offs and I can't say I blame them. This is a great mix of smooth goat cheese, tangy cranberries, and crunchy almonds for a mixture that's amazing to the senses.

BALSAMIC VINAIGRETTE
- ½ cup balsamic vinegar
- 2 tablespoons Dijon mustard
- 2 tablespoons honey
- 1 large egg yolk
- 1 cup extra virgin olive oil

SALAD
- 1 cup blanched sliced almonds
- 1 8-ounce log goat cheese
- 1 cup all-purpose flour
- 3 large eggs, well beaten
- 1 cup plain breadcrumbs
- 1 cup canola oil for frying
- 1 tablespoon sea salt, plus more for sprinkling
- 1 tablespoon freshly ground black pepper, plus more for sprinkling
- 1 head iceberg lettuce
- ½ pound mixed greens
- 1 cup thinly sliced red onion
- 1 cup dried cranberries
- 1 bunch fresh thyme, chopped

To make the dressing, add the vinegar, mustard, honey, and yolk to a food processor or blender and blend to combine. With the motor running, drizzle in the oil slowly at first, then add in a thin, steady stream until all the oil is added and the mixture is smooth. Refrigerate until ready to use.

To make the salad, preheat the oven to 350°F. Spread the almonds out on a baking sheet in a single layer. Toast for about 5 minutes, or until golden brown. Remove and cool.

Cut the goat cheese into eight 1-ounce rounds. Dredge each piece in flour, dip in the beaten eggs, and coat in breadcrumbs. Line a plate with paper towels.

Meanwhile, heat the oil in a large skillet over medium heat. Fry the goat cheese slices until golden brown on both sides, about 1 minute on each side. Remove with a slotted spoon. Drain on the paper towels. Sprinkle with salt and pepper.

Remove the root end from the lettuce, and cut the head into 4 wedges. Place one wedge each on four individual serving dishes. Scatter the mixed greens around each wedge. Dress each wedge with 2 tablespoons of the dressing, some of the 1 tablespoon sea salt, and some of the 1 tablespoon pepper. Top with almonds, onion, cranberries, and thyme. Garnish each salad with 2 goat cheese slices.

SOME
SALADS
ARE
SHOW-OFFS

FENNEL, ORANGE, AND
POMEGRANATE WEDGE (SERVES 4)

These are what I like to call money ingredients. A perfect aphrodisiac meal with vibrant colors—sexy, luminous, and fresh!

If you cannot find fresh pomegranates because of the season, use dried cranberries instead.

CITRUS VINAIGRETTE
- ½ cup fresh orange juice
- ½ cup diced red onion
- 2 tablespoons honey
- 2 tablespoons Dijon mustard
- 1 teaspoon sea salt
- 1 teaspoon freshly ground black pepper
- ½ teaspoon crushed red pepper
- 1 cup extra virgin olive oil

SALAD
- 1 head iceberg lettuce
- ½ pound mixed greens
- 1 large fennel bulb, thinly sliced
- 2 blood oranges, peeled and sliced into ¼-inch-thick rounds
- ½ cup thinly sliced red onion
- ½ cup chopped fresh mint
- Seeds from ½ pomegranate, or ½ cup dried cranberries

To make the vinaigrette, add the orange juice, onion, honey, mustard, salt, black pepper, and crushed red pepper to a food processor or blender and blend to combine. With the motor running, drizzle in the oil slowly at first, then add in a thin, steady stream until all the oil is added and the mixture is smooth. Set aside until ready to use.

To make the salad, remove the root end from the lettuce and cut the head into 4 wedges. Place one wedge each on four individual serving dishes. Mix the mixed greens with the fennel and scatter around each wedge. Dress each wedge with 2 tablespoons of the dressing. Top with orange, onion, mint, and pomegranate seeds.

ARUGULA, RED ONION, AND
PARMESAN WEDGE (SERVES 4)

When less is best, this is an elegant salad that pleases everyone's palate. You can't go wrong serving this at large dinner parties—it's basic but delicious.

LEMON VINAIGRETTE
- ½ cup fresh lemon juice
- 2 tablespoons honey
- 1 teaspoon sea salt
- 1 teaspoon freshly ground black pepper
- 1 cup extra virgin olive oil

SALAD
- 1 head iceberg lettuce
- ½ pound fresh arugula
  Sea salt
  Freshly ground black pepper
- 1 cup pine nuts, optional
- 1 red onion, thinly sliced
- 8 ounces Parmesan cheese, shaved

To make the vinaigrette, add the lemon juice, honey, salt, and pepper to a food processor or blender and blend to combine. With the motor running, drizzle in the oil slowly at first, then add in a thin, steady stream until all the oil is added and the mixture is smooth. Set aside until ready to use.

To make the salad, remove the root end from the lettuce, and cut the head into 4 wedges. Place one wedge each on four individual serving dishes. Scatter the arugula around each wedge. Dress each wedge with 2 tablespoons of the dressing and salt and pepper to taste. Top with the pine nuts, onion, and Parmesan.

POACHED EGGS AND
FRISÉE WEDGE (SERVES 4)

Poached or fried egg on anything is magical. It's my favorite way to tweak a traditional dish, and the classic French chefs had it right when they came up with this one. Needless to say, this salad has "moi" written all over it. You will need a shallow saucepan with a lid and a slotted spoon for poaching the eggs.

WARM SHERRY VINAIGRETTE
- ½ cup sherry vinegar
- ½ cup chopped red onion
- 2 tablespoons whole-grain mustard
- 2 tablespoons honey
- 1 garlic clove
- 1 teaspoon sea salt
- 1 teaspoon freshly ground black pepper
- 1 cup grapeseed oil

SALAD
- 1 pound applewood-smoked bacon
- 1 head iceberg lettuce
- 1 pound frisée
- 1 cup thinly sliced red onion
- ½ cup thinly sliced scallions

POACHED EGGS
- 4 large eggs
- 1 to 2 teaspoons rice vinegar

To make the vinaigrette, add the vinegar, onion, mustard, honey, garlic, salt, and pepper to a food processor or blender and blend to combine. With the motor running, drizzle in the oil slowly at first, then add in a thin, steady stream until all the oil is added and the mixture is smooth. Set aside until ready to use. Just before dressing the lettuce, heat the vinaigrette in a saucepan over medium heat for 2 minutes.

To make the salad, heat a skillet over medium heat and cook the bacon until crisp. Line a metal tray with paper towels. Drain the bacon. Cool, crumble, and set aside.

Remove the root end from the lettuce and cut the head into 4 wedges. Place one wedge each on four individual serving dishes. Scatter the frisée around each wedge. Dress each wedge with 2 tablespoons of the dressing. Top with the bacon, onion, and scallions.

To poach the eggs, line a plate with paper towels. Fill a medium saucepan ¾ of the way up with water and bring to a simmer, then add 1 to 2 teaspoons vinegar. Crack an egg into a small cup and gently slide it into the water. Using a slotted spoon, nudge the egg white closer to the yolk. When the white is cooked, carefully remove the egg from the water. Drain on the paper towels. Repeat with the remaining eggs. Top each salad with an egg before serving.

ASIAN PEAR, PISTACHIO, AND
BRIE WEDGE (SERVES 4)

An ambitious salad certain to start the meal off with a bang. Make sure you get a great recommendation from your local cheese specialist. A divine Brie is the key ingredient—soft, fierce, and perfect to the tongue. I love you, Brie.

RASPBERRY VINAIGRETTE
- ½ cup seedless raspberry preserves
- ½ cup red wine vinegar
- 2 tablespoons honey
- 1 garlic clove, minced
- 1 tablespoon fresh lemon juice
- 1 teaspoon sea salt
- 1 teaspoon freshly ground black pepper
- 1 cup grapeseed oil

SALAD
- 1 head iceberg lettuce
- ½ pound mixed greens
- 1 Asian pear, cut in half, cored, and thinly sliced in half circles
- 1 Granny Smith apple, cut in half, cored, and thinly sliced in half circles
- 1 red apple, cut in half, cored, and thinly sliced in half circles
- 1 cup shelled pistachios, chopped
- 1 red onion, thinly sliced
- 1 8-ounce wheel Brie, cut into slices and softened at room temperature

To make the vinaigrette, add the preserves, vinegar, honey, garlic, lemon juice, salt, and pepper to a food processor or blender and blend to combine. With the motor running, drizzle in the oil slowly at first, then add in a thin, steady stream until all the oil is added and the mixture is smooth. Set aside until ready to use.

To make the salad, remove the root end from the lettuce and cut the head into 4 wedges. Place one wedge each on four individual serving dishes. Scatter the mixed greens around each wedge. Dress each wedge with 2 tablespoons of the dressing. Top with the pear, apples, pistachios, and onion. Place slices of the Brie around each wedge.

ERR ON THE SIDE OF . . . SIDES

3

SUNNY'S HAND-CUT FRIES
SPIKE'S VILLAGE FRIES
CLIFF'S HOMEGROWN VIDALIA ONION PETALS
UNCLE D'S CHILI
CHEDDAR CHEESE SAUCE
NIC'S MESS WITH SUNNY'S HAND-CUT FRIES
BAKED SWEET POTATO FRIES
STREET-STYLE CORN ON THE COB
ZUCCHINI FRITTERS
HOMEMADE CORNBREAD
BIG B'S BAKED BEANS
RED CABBAGE SLAW
FARM-FRESH POTATO SALAD
MAC 'N' CHEESE
ROASTED CORN AND RED PEPPER SALSA
PEPERONATA
FRESH FRUIT SALAD
FRIED BRUSSELS SPROUTS
CELERY ROOT, POTATO, AND PEAR GRATIN
BACON-WRAPPED ASPARAGUS
GRILLED WATERMELON, YUZU, AND FETA SALAD
PERFECTLY ROASTED WILD MUSHROOMS

I might be a front 'n' center kind of guy, but that doesn't mean some of my recipes can't be the sidekick or the **wingman**! A well-prepared side dish can be the best thing to happen to a meal. How many times have you moaned over crisp, perfectly seasoned **french fries**, or practically jumped into a vat of potato salad? Sides, with their quiet confidence, can be mind-blowing, and even a ham like me can admit it.

SUNNY'S
HAND-CUT FRIES (SERVES 4)

When my grandfather Sunny was little, he babysat his siblings: Paul, Philip, Maggie, Helen, and Barbara. His sister Helen still talks about how exciting it was when Sunny was in charge, because as soon as their parents left, he'd make french fries and serve them all in one huge brown paper bag. So in our home, we've always served them in paper bags.

5 pounds Red Bliss
   potatoes (see Note)
   Canola oil for
   deep-frying

Sea salt and freshly
ground black pepper

Wash and scrub the potatoes under cold running water. Pat dry with paper towels. Cut into rectangular strips about ⅜ inch thick. Rinse the potato strips in cold water for about 2 minutes. Drain.

In a deep pot or deep-fat fryer, heat about 2½ inches of oil until a thermometer reads 250°F. Line a metal tray or baking sheet with paper towels.

Add one handful of the potatoes to the pot. Fry until tender but have no color, about 3½ minutes. Remove with a slotted spoon. Drain on the paper towels. Repeat until all the strips are cooked. Refrigerate until cool.

Reheat the oil to 350°F. Line the metal tray with fresh paper towels.

Add the cooled potatoes a few handfuls at a time and fry them until golden and crispy. Remove with a slotted spoon. Drain on the paper towels. Season with salt and pepper while the strips are still hot. Serve immediately.

NOTE

Red Bliss potatoes are light-skinned potatoes. They cook faster and are sweeter than Russet or Idaho potatoes. Their tender skin is edible.

FRYING STATION

Frying is an art, and you must do it safely and properly. When you fry something, like our hand-cut fries, your goal is a great brown crisp outside that surrounds something wonderful and soft on the inside.

A FEW KEY STEPS:

- You'll need a deep-frying pan since it requires at least 2½ inches of oil. You can use a wok or a pot as well.
- A slotted spoon is essential. It allows you to place the food in the hot oil and pick it back up without having puddles of oil around your food.
- The best frying oil is one with a high smoke point, which is the temperature to which an oil can be heated before it smokes and discolors. It's going to fry the potato quicker, making it crispier on the outside while keeping the inside of the potato tender and moist. The oil takes a longer time to smoke, allowing for the best frying quality. Some oils I like to use are peanut, sunflower, grapeseed, and canola.
- Make sure you are very careful when you deep-fry—don't fill your fryer more than halfway with the oil.
- Heat the oil to between 350° and 375°F. Any lower and the food will absorb oil and become soggy instead of being light and crisp. Any higher and the outside will burn while the inside remains uncooked. The blanching temperature is 220°F, and regular frying is 350° to 375°F.
- Most foods need to be breaded or battered before you fry them. While the oil is heating, prepare the batter. For others, however, such as the LouKou Beignets on page 234, you place the batter directly into your hot oil.

- Place the food you're frying into the oil using a slotted spoon, submerging it gradually if possible. You do not want to spatter the hot oil.
- Do not overcrowd the pot. You don't want your items to bump into each other as they cook.
- Follow recipe instructions, but also pay attention to the food. When it's golden brown, it's probably done.
- Once the frying is complete, place your food on a paper towel–lined plate and pat dry.
- If you're frying a large amount, place the first batches in a 200°F oven while you keep frying.
- Do not reuse any vegetable oil used for frying in other nonfrying recipes. Only reserve this oil if you plan to use it again for frying.
- Once it is cooled, strain the oil and place it in a milk container or something with a tight top, away from light.
- If your oil turns dark or starts to smell, get rid of it. Put the container in the garbage.

DO NOT POUR IT DOWN THE DRAIN

SPIKE'S
VILLAGE FRIES (SERVES 4)

One of my favorite things is walking through a farmers' market and smelling all the wonderful fruits, herbs, and spices of local farmers. I love going to that part of the market where you find fresh rosemary, thyme, sage, basil, and oregano—it's a feast for your nose! These fries came out of the passion of fresh herbs and the perfect french fry.

5 pounds Red Bliss potatoes	1 cup chopped fresh rosemary
Canola oil for deep-frying	1 cup chopped fresh thyme
	¼ cup sea salt

Wash and scrub potatoes under cold running water. Pat dry with paper towels. Cut in half lengthwise, then into long strips about ¼-inch thick.

In a deep pot or deep-fat fryer, heat about 3 inches of oil until a thermometer reads 250°F. Line a metal tray or baking sheet with paper towels.

Add one handful of the potatoes to the pot. Fry until tender but have no color. Remove with a slotted spoon. Drain on the paper towels. Repeat the procedure until all the strips are cooked. Refrigerate until cool.

Reheat the oil to 350°F. Line the metal tray with fresh paper towels.

Add the cooled potatoes a few handfuls at a time and fry until golden and crispy. Remove with a slotted spoon. Drain on the paper towels. Toss with the rosemary, thyme, and salt while the slices are still hot. Serve immediately.

THE ONION HOW-TO

Cut approximately ¾ inch off of the top and bottom of the onion and remove the skin. Using a large, sharp knife, slice down the center of the onion. Keep slicing the sections in half until you have 8 wedges. Spread the petals apart to coat evenly.

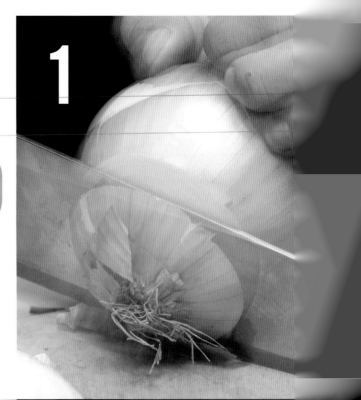

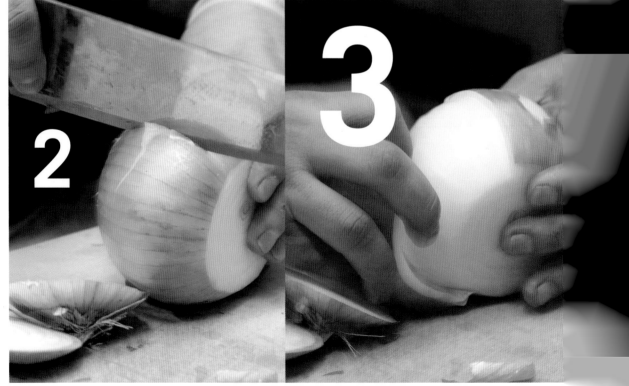

MAKING
PETALS

4

5

CLIFF'S HOMEGROWN VIDALIA ONION PETALS (SERVES 4)

My brother-in-law Cliff grew up in Vidalia, Georgia. When we started talking about the menu for the restaurant, he was adamant about onion petals . . . from Vidalia. There wasn't an option to use anything else. In fact, when Cliff's parents, Wesley and Jan Luhn, came to the restaurant, I knew everything would be smooth sailing because they had tasted the petals and approved. The Luhns are the best ambassadors for Vidalia and the onions truly are delicious.

ONION RING BATTER (can be made 1 day in advance)
- 2 cups all-purpose flour
- 1 tablespoon sea salt
- 1 tablespoon Hungarian paprika
- 1 tablespoon light brown sugar
- 1½ teaspoons Old Bay seasoning
- 1 teaspoon ground cumin
- Pinch freshly ground black pepper
- Pinch ground cayenne
- 1 cup beer (any kind you like)
- 1 cup buttermilk
- 1 large egg, beaten

ONION PETALS
- Canola oil for deep-frying
- 1 cup all-purpose flour
- 4 Vidalia onions, each cut into 8 wedges (petals)
- Sea salt and freshly ground black pepper

To make the onion ring batter, into a large bowl, sift the flour, salt, paprika, brown sugar, Old Bay seasoning, cumin, black pepper, and cayenne. In another large bowl, combine the beer, buttermilk, and egg. Slowly incorporate the dry ingredients into the wet, whisking to prevent lumps. Refrigerate until needed.

To make the onion petals, in a large, deep skillet, heat about 3 inches of oil until a thermometer reads 350°F. Line a metal tray with paper towels.

Add the flour to a bowl. Add the onions and toss, coating them well. Shake off the excess. Dip the petals into the batter and coat well. Carefully add the petals, one by one, to the hot oil, making sure not to overcrowd the skillet. Fry until golden brown and crispy. Remove with a slotted spoon. Drain on the paper towels. Season with salt and pepper while still hot. Serve immediately.

ANYTHING ELSE IS NOT AN OPTION

UNCLE D'S
CHILI (SERVES 4)

If anyone in this business could make money out of a stone, it was Uncle Denny. He had a club called the Blue Angel, which had a lab downstairs where he mixed bootleg liquor with legal liquor. He knew how to get the absolute most out of anything. He's been credited with watering down mustard, not giving lids or straws on cups, and telling people he's out of napkins when he had a whole supply stashed away. But his absolute best was whenever a cook was ready to pitch something, he'd look at it and say, "Put it in the chili!" It became a family joke, so how could we not name it after Uncle D!

32 ounces ground beef
 2 tablespoons canola oil
 1 cup diced red onion
 1 green bell pepper, seeded and diced
 1 16-ounce can kidney beans, drained and rinsed

 1 tablespoon ground cumin
 2 tablespoons Hungarian paprika
 1 tablespoon chili powder
 1 tablespoon freshly ground black pepper
 1 32-ounce can tomato sauce

 1 cup Chipotle-Barbecue Sauce (page 132)
 Sea salt
 ½ cup Cheddar Cheese Sauce (page 87)
 ½ cup sour cream

Heat the beef in a large skillet over medium heat. Cook, stirring and breaking it up, until browned. Drain off the fat. Heat the oil in another large skillet over medium-low heat. Add the onion and green pepper and cook, stirring, until softened and the onion is translucent, about 10 minutes. Add the beans, cumin, paprika, chili powder, and black pepper. Increase the heat to medium and cook, stirring, until the mixture is fragrant, about 4 minutes.

Add the browned beef and continue cooking and stirring until well mixed. Add the tomato sauce and 1 cup of water, and reduce the heat to medium-low. Cook, stirring occasionally, until the mixture thickens, about 1 hour. Stir in the Chipotle-Barbecue Sauce and season with salt. Top each serving with a tablespoon each of Cheddar Cheese Sauce and sour cream. Serve immediately.

"SILKY, SMOOTH, MOUTHWATERING"

CHEDDAR CHEESE
SAUCE (MAKES 3 CUPS)

There's always a reason to have cheddar cheese sauce on hand—everything goes with it. Warm, oozing cheese is never a bad idea.

2 cups whole milk
¼ cup (½ stick) unsalted
   butter
1 cup all-purpose flour
1 cup grated sharp
   cheddar cheese

1½ teaspoons ground
   cayenne
Sea salt and freshly
   ground black pepper

Heat the milk in a large saucepan over medium heat until you see bubbles forming on top. Meanwhile, melt the butter in another saucepan and stir in the flour to make a roux (see Note). Add the warm milk, whisking constantly, and continue cooking until the mixture thickens, about 5 minutes. Add the cheese, whisking constantly to combine. Season with the cayenne and salt and pepper to taste. Strain through a sieve to remove any lumps before serving.

NOTE

A roux, used in classical French cuisine, is a mixture of flour and fat, usually butter or oil.

NIC'S MESS WITH SUNNY'S
HAND-CUT FRIES (SERVES 4)

This kid knows way too much about me. I grew up with Nic Georgeades—another Greek, of course—on Clearwater Beach, Florida. We both worked on the beach at this famous hotel called Shepard's, renting out jet skis, getting tourists chairs, serving drinks behind the bar. I think we did everything illegal we possibly could and survived to tell the tale . . . but only barely. Nic and I have been scheming since I was about 14 years old, and our biggest dream when we were kids was to build a restaurant empire together.

I had been living in D.C. for all of three weeks, starting to put the crew for the Good Stuff Eatery together. So I called him. I think the phone call went something like: "Yo, the time has come—get your ass to D.C."

And so a week later Nic was in D.C. living with my sister and her husband in their guest room. My Food and Beverage Operations Manager had arrived!

1 recipe Sunny's Hand-Cut
   Fries (page 71)
1 recipe Uncle D's Chili
   (page 84)
1 cup sour cream

1 cup Cheddar Cheese
   Sauce (page 87)
4 teaspoons minced fresh
   scallions

Place a handful of fries into each of four serving bowls. Spoon chili over the fries and top with sour cream, cheese sauce, and a sprinkling of chives. Serve immediately.

BAKED SWEET POTATO
FRIES (SERVES 4)

My grandmother, who we call Zas, is not really the grandmotherly sort. She looks half her age—always with the latest makeup, perfect jewelry, and fashionable outfits with shoes and purse to match. Among her many refined qualities, Zas is a complete sweet potato junkie, this is a must-have when she comes to visit.

4 sweet potatoes,
    unpeeled and cut into
    wedges
¼ cup chopped fresh sage
½ cup packed light brown
    sugar

½ cup extra virgin olive oil
    Sea salt and freshly
    ground black pepper

Preheat the oven to 350°F.

In a large bowl, combine the sweet potatoes, sage, brown sugar, and oil. Season with salt and pepper, and toss. Spread on a baking sheet. Bake for 40 minutes. Serve immediately.

STREET-STYLE CORN
ON THE COB (SERVES 4)

Corn on the cob gives me such nostalgia, it's nutso. I'm always fascinated by how some foods can do that—just bring you right back to the moment you first tasted them. I vividly remember landing in Vietnam with my friend Colletti to start a few months of culinary adventuring on behalf of Drew Nieporent and Michael Huynh for the new Vietnamese restaurant we were preparing to open. We were there to gather recipes and learn how to do Vietnamese cooking right. We were famished. We were disoriented. We didn't smell too great. Just as we hopped a bus going who-knows-where, a corn on the cob cart caught our eye. Like vultures, we bounced off the bus and bought ourselves the most mouthwatering ears of corn we had ever had. Baked in butter and Parmesan, you couldn't ask for a better first meal to kick off an unforgettable journey!

You can grill these on an outdoor barbecue or broil them in the oven.

4 ears fresh corn	2 scallions, thinly sliced	½ red onion, diced
Canola oil for brushing, plus 1 tablespoon	¼ cup Chipotle Mayonnaise (page 36)	Chopped fresh cilantro for garnish
Sea salt and freshly ground black pepper	Freshly grated Parmesan cheese	

Preheat the grill until smoking hot. Brush the corn with the oil and season with salt and pepper. Place on the grill and char the corn on all sides, about 3 minutes on each side, or until you see the corn getting charred.

Meanwhile, heat the 1 tablespoon oil in a skillet over medium heat. Add the scallions and cook for about 30 seconds. Season with salt and set aside.

When the corn is tender, spread 1 tablespoon mayonnaise on each ear and sprinkle with the Parmesan, onion, and scallions. Garnish with the cilantro. Serve immediately.

ZUCCHINI FRITTERS (SERVES 4)

When you grow up with a Greek mother, zucchini fritters become everyday, all-day snacks, especially when you grow zucchini in your garden, as we do at our villa in Kefalonia. I like to say they're the ethnic equivalent of potato chips . . . but so much better!

- 9 large eggs, beaten
- 4 tablespoons extra virgin olive oil
- 3 tablespoons freshly grated Parmesan
- cheese
- 1 tablespoon sea salt, plus more
- Freshly ground black pepper
- ½ cup all-purpose flour
- ½ cup plain breadcrumbs
- 2 large zucchini, grated
- Canola oil for frying

In a mixing bowl, beat the eggs, olive oil, Parmesan, the 1 tablespoon salt, and some pepper. Slowly mix in the flour and breadcrumbs. Fold in the grated zucchini. Cover and refrigerate for 30 minutes.

In a large pot, heat about 3 inches of oil over medium heat until it starts to sizzle. Meanwhile, line a baking sheet with paper towels.

Remove the batter from the refrigerator and carefully add it, one spoonful at a time, to the hot oil. Cook each fritter until golden brown all over, 5 to 10 minutes. Remove with a slotted spoon. Drain on the paper towels. Season with salt and pepper. Serve immediately.

HOMEMADE
CORNBREAD (SERVES 8)

I could eat this every day for the rest of my life. There's nothing like a warm piece of cornbread out of the oven, sliced in half with a piece of butter, melting ever so softly as the heat escapes and it melts in your mouth.

1½ cups yellow cornmeal
1½ cups all-purpose flour
½ cup honey
3 teaspoons baking
   powder

1 scant teaspoon sea salt
½ teaspoon baking soda
1¼ cups buttermilk
1 14-ounce can sweetened
   condensed milk

1 cup canned creamed
   corn, optional
2 large eggs
6 tablespoons (¾ stick)
   unsalted butter, melted

Preheat the oven to 400°F. Grease and flour a 9-inch square baking pan.

In a mixing bowl, combine the cornmeal, flour, honey, baking powder, salt, and baking soda. In another bowl, whisk together the buttermilk, condensed milk, creamed corn, if using, eggs, and melted butter. Incorporate the wet ingredients into the dry, stirring to prevent lumps. Spread the batter into the prepared pan.

Bake for 30 to 35 minutes, or until lightly browned and firm. Slice while still warm and enjoy.

BIG B'S
BAKED BEANS
(SERVES 4)

B stands for Brian. Brian is the Man. He's another buddy I brought to Good Stuff from New York, and let me tell you, we'd absolutely crumble without him. He's god of the grill, the sounding board for all our b-tching and moaning, and above all, a decent man and devoted friend who never so much as mumbles a complaint (even on our worst, 17-hour, if-I-see-another hamburger-I'm-going-to-shoot-myself days). These are his beans.

1 pound applewood-smoked bacon, chopped (about 2 cups)
1 small white onion, diced
1 cup tomato sauce, or 1 cup canned peeled tomatoes

½ cup packed light brown sugar
2 tablespoons molasses
1 tablespoon cayenne
½ cup apple cider vinegar
2 32-ounce cans white beans, drained and rinsed

1 cup Chipotle-Barbecue Sauce (page 132)

Preheat the oven to 350°F. Line a metal tray with paper towels.

Heat a large skillet over medium heat and cook the bacon until crisp. Remove with a slotted spoon. Drain the bacon on the paper towels.

Add the onion to the bacon fat in the pan and cook, stirring, until translucent, about 3 minutes. Add the tomato sauce and bring the mixture to a boil. Add the brown sugar, molasses, and cayenne and stir until well combined. Add the vinegar and stir to combine, scraping the bottom of the skillet to loosen any remaining bits of bacon. Add the beans, sauce, and bacon and heat through.

Spoon the mixture into a 3-quart ovenproof dish and cover with foil. Bake for 30 minutes, or until the mixture is thick and bubbly.

RED CABBAGE
SLAW (SERVES 4)

This is what I like to call my slammin' slaw. It turns your traditional slaw into something you'll never touch or make again. The raisins and apples add a sweet flavor to the pickled carrots and daikon, and the mustard and vinegar bring it home.

1 cup red wine vinegar
½ cup sugar
2 tablespoons whole-grain mustard
2 teaspoons ground cinnamon
1 head red cabbage, cored and shredded
1 cup dark raisins

1 cup thinly sliced red onion
1 cup pickled carrots (page 138)
1 cup pickled daikon (page 138)
2 green apples, cored and julienned

1½ cups Homemade Basic Mayonnaise (page 34)
1 cup coarsely chopped fresh mint
Sea salt and freshly ground black pepper

In a bowl, whisk together the vinegar, sugar, mustard, and cinnamon until well combined. Add the cabbage, raisins, and onion and toss. Fold in the carrots, daikon, apples, and mayonnaise. Add the mint and season with salt and pepper.

Serve immediately or refrigerate for no more than ½ hour. The slaw will get soggy if stored longer.

FARM-FRESH POTATO
SALAD (SERVES 4)

Who doesn't love potato salad? If you raised your hand, we can't be friends.
Here's a fresh, basic recipe that goes with any meal. You can make this one day ahead.

5 pounds Red Bliss
 potatoes, washed and
 each cut into eighths
 Sea salt
2 cups Homemade Basic
 Mayonnaise (page 34)
1 cup sherry vinegar

½ cup extra virgin olive oil
2 tablespoons whole-grain
 mustard
1 small red onion, diced
2 stalks celery, chopped
5 garlic cloves, crushed
1 bunch fresh thyme,
 chopped

1 bunch fresh parsley,
 chopped
 Freshly ground black
 pepper

Put the potatoes in a large pot over high heat, cover with water, and season with salt. Bring to a boil, reduce the heat to low, and cook until the potatoes are fork tender, 15 to 20 minutes. Drain and set aside to cool.

Meanwhile, in a large bowl, stir together the mayonnaise, vinegar, oil, and mustard until well combined. Add the onion, celery, and garlic and mix until well combined. When the potatoes are cool enough to handle, cube them and add to the bowl. Add the thyme and parsley, season with salt and pepper, and toss. Serve immediately.

"THIS AIN'T NO STORE-BOUGHT MAC 'N' CHEESE"

MAC 'N' CHEESE (SERVES 4)

It's impossible not to love mac 'n' cheese. It's not only the ultimate comfort food, but everyone has a great memory of eating it—either out of the box or made from scratch—and savoring every single bite. Most American-food cookbooks have a version of this classic, and this one is mine. It's creamy, filled with rosemary, thyme, and sage (three of my favorite herbs), and topped off with panko breadcrumbs, which give it a nice crunchy bite.

- Butter for the baking dish
- 1 pound elbow macaroni
- 2 teaspoons sea salt
- 2 tablespoons extra virgin olive oil
- 1 cup Cheddar Cheese Sauce (page 87)
- 10 slices bacon
- 2 cups freshly grated Parmesan cheese
- 1½ cups panko breadcrumbs
- ½ cup minced fresh parsley
- 1 tablespoon minced fresh thyme
- 1 tablespoon minced fresh rosemary
- 1 teaspoon minced fresh sage
- 2 tablespoons freshly ground black pepper

Preheat the oven to 375°F. Grease a 3-quart ovenproof baking dish with butter, and set aside.

Bring water to a boil in a large saucepan over high heat. Add the macaroni and salt, reduce to medium heat, and stir to prevent sticking. Cook for 7 minutes, or until al dente. Drain and toss with the oil.

Heat the cheese sauce in a saucepan over medium heat. In a skillet, cook the bacon over medium heat until crisp. Line a metal tray with paper towels. Drain the bacon. Chop the bacon into bits.

In a bowl, combine the bacon, Parmesan, 1 cup of the breadcrumbs, the parsley, thyme, rosemary, sage, and pepper. In another bowl, toss together the macaroni and heated cheese sauce, mixing well. Stir the macaroni-cheese mixture into the breadcrumbs mixture. Spread evenly into the prepared baking dish, and sprinkle with the remaining ½ cup breadcrumbs.

Place the baking dish on top of a baking pan to catch spills if the cheese bubbles over. Bake for 40 minutes, or until crispy and brown on top.

ROASTED CORN AND
RED PEPPER SALSA (SERVES 4)

When corn is in season, it's like candy, and you want to do everything humanly possible to incorporate it into your meals. This is refreshing and simple, with an extra "chef-y" twist that will enhance every dish . . . from chips to salads to swordfish.

2 ears fresh corn or one 16-ounce can corn
1 tablespoon extra virgin olive oil
Sea salt

1 small red bell pepper, seeded and diced
½ red onion, diced
½ cup chopped fresh cilantro

1 scallion, sliced
½ cup white wine vinegar
2 tablespoons sugar
Freshly ground black pepper

Carefully remove the kernels from the cobs. The best way to do this is to hold an ear by the tip and stand it upright on the stem end in a bowl. Cut down the sides of the cob with a sharp knife, releasing the kernels without cutting into the cob.

Heat the oil in a skillet over medium heat until smoking. Add the kernels and cook, stirring, until nicely crisp, about 10 minutes. Season with salt and set aside to cool.

When ready to serve, combine the corn, red pepper, onion, cilantro, scallion, vinegar, and sugar. Mix well and season with salt and pepper. Serve immediately.

PEPERONATA (SERVES 4)

The best thing about peperonata? Longevity. Awesome to have in the fridge for late-night nibbles and pick-me-ups for the week. This recipe has a nice kick to it.

4½ teaspoons extra virgin olive oil

1 red onion, thinly sliced

1 red bell pepper, seeded and julienned

1 orange bell pepper, seeded and julienned

1 yellow bell pepper, seeded and julienned

1 tablespoon sea salt, plus more to taste

¾ cup sugar

¾ cup red wine vinegar

Pinch crushed red pepper

Freshly ground black pepper

Heat the oil in a large skillet over medium heat. Add the red onion and cook, stirring, until translucent, about 3 minutes. Add the bell peppers and 1 tablespoon salt and cook, stirring often to prevent browning, 20 to 25 minutes. Stir in the sugar and vinegar and cook until the mixture thickens, about 5 minutes more. Season with salt, crushed red pepper, and black pepper. Cool and reserve for later use.

FRESH FRUIT
SALAD (SERVES 4)

I consider fresh fruit one of life's greatest gems. I'm smiling just imagining the fresh bowls of oranges on our breakfast table. I really have never tasted fresher fruit than in Greece, and even today my mouth waters at the memories of driving in Greece with my family, stopping by the side of the road, plucking the fruit, washing it with my bottle of water, and biting into it.

2 cups seedless red grapes
2 cups seedless green grapes
2 cups diced Granny Smith apple
2 cups sliced kiwi

2 cups sliced banana
2 cups diced pineapple
½ cup Greek yogurt, or any thick, creamy, plain yogurt
4 tablespoons honey

1 cup chopped fresh mint
½ cup chopped fresh cilantro
Juice from 1 lemon

In a large bowl, combine the grapes, apple, kiwi, banana, and pineapple. In another bowl, stir together the yogurt, honey, mint, cilantro, and lemon juice until well combined. Pour over the fruit and gently toss without bruising the fruit. Serve immediately.

FRIED BRUSSELS
SPROUTS (SERVES 4)

I never, ever ever ate Brussels sprouts while I was growing up. Most kids squirm at the thought, and I was definitely one of them. That is, until I did 'em up Spike-style! Fried with bacon, Brussels sprouts go from zero to hero real fast. Trust me, you'll never squirm again.

- 1 pound Brussels sprouts
  Canola oil for frying
- 1 cup coarsely chopped
  fresh mint leaves
- 2 teaspoons sea salt
- 2 teaspoons freshly ground
  black pepper
- 1 teaspoon crushed red
  pepper
  Juice from 1 lemon

Trim the ends off the Brussels sprouts and remove and reserve the outer leaves. Wash the separated outer leaves and whole Brussels sprouts thoroughly in cold water. Drain, and set aside. The separated outer leaves can be saved for a salad or another dish.

Heat about 3 inches of the oil in a large saucepan over medium heat. When the oil begins to smoke, carefully add the sprouts and cook them for about 4 minutes, or until golden brown and crispy. Remove with a slotted spoon. Place in a bowl. Add the mint leaves, salt, black pepper, crushed red pepper, and lemon juice to the bowl and toss to coat the sprouts evenly. Serve immediately.

CELERY ROOT, POTATO, AND PEAR GRATIN (SERVES 4)

All you need to do is get a fantastic fire going and curl up on the couch with a blanket, wine, and this gratin.

Butter for the baking dish

6 tablespoons extra virgin olive oil

1 pound celery root, peeled, quartered, and sliced ¼ inch thick

1 pound Red Bliss potatoes

½ pound Bartlett pears

¾ cup heavy cream

1 garlic clove, peeled and smashed

1 cup grated Gruyère cheese

⅔ cup grated Parmesan cheese

1 teaspoon chopped fresh thyme

2 teaspoons sea salt, plus more for sprinkling

2 teaspoons freshly ground black pepper, plus more for sprinkling

Preheat the oven to 375°F. Grease a 9-by-13-inch baking dish with butter and set aside. Line a plate with paper towels.

Heat 2 tablespoons of the oil in a large skillet over medium heat. Add the celery root to the skillet. Cook until browned on both sides, about 10 minutes total. Remove with a slotted spoon. Drain on the paper towels.

Meanwhile, peel and slice the potatoes ¼ inch thick. Add 2 more tablespoons of oil to the skillet and add the potatoes. Cook until browned and tender, about 10 minutes. Remove with a slotted spoon. Drain on the paper towels with the celery root. Repeat this procedure with the pears, adding 2 more tablespoons of oil, cooking for 10 minutes, and draining them on the paper towels. Season the celery root, potato, and pear with salt and pepper.

Heat the cream and garlic in a saucepan over medium-high heat. In a bowl, combine the cheeses, thyme, the 2 teaspoons salt, and the 2 teaspoons pepper.

Layer the celery root to cover the bottom of the prepared baking dish. Sprinkle a third of the cheese mixture over it. Pour a quarter of the cream mixture on top. Layer the potatoes, sprinkle the second third of the cheese mixture on top, and pour the second quarter of the cream over it. Top off with the pears and sprinkle the last third of the cheese mixture on top for an extra-thick coating. Pour the remaining cream mixture over everything. Cover with foil.

Bake for 30 minutes, then uncover and bake for 20 minutes more, or until bubbling and browned on top. Let cool for 15 minutes before serving.

BACON-WRAPPED
ASPARAGUS (SERVES 4)

We often sit for a family-style dinner, in our restaurant, that starts when we close. One night, the crew and fam got together for a Christmas dinner before everyone left for the holiday. We made an amazing bone marrow dish, roasted garlic-and-rosemary fillet of beef, beet salad with goat cheese and mint, cauliflower au gratin . . . the menu was endless (and incredible). It wasn't supposed to be such a big deal, but by the time 11 P.M. rolled around, it was. Colletti's contribution was these amazing bundles of joy. It's all about the bacon.

20 asparagus spears
5 slices bacon
   Sea salt and freshly
      ground black pepper
2 teaspoons canola oil

¼ cup Lemon Vinaigrette
   (page 62)

Trim the asparagus spears from the bottom end so they are about 5 inches long. Lay a slice of bacon flat on a cutting board, and place 5 spears on one end. Roll the bacon around the bundle of asparagus. Season with salt and pepper.

Heat the oil in a large skillet over medium heat. Line a large plate with paper towels.

Place the wrapped asparagus in the skillet and cook, turning as needed, until the bacon is crisp. Remove with a slotted spoon (or a pair of tongs). Drain on the paper towels. Transfer to a serving dish and drizzle with Lemon Vinaigrette. Serve immediately.

GRILLED WATERMELON, YUZU, AND FETA SALAD (SERVES 4)

A Japanese citrus fruit, the yuzu has a sour taste but an aromatic rind. Its juice is favored in drinks and as a flavoring. Look for yuzu juice in specialty Japanese or Asian markets. You will need only one-quarter of a watermelon for this recipe, so save the rest for other uses. Try to use Bulgarian feta, an excellent rich and creamy sheep's milk cheese. This cheese is much stronger, saltier, and creamier than other feta cheeses.

¼ of a large watermelon
½ cup yuzu juice
2 tablespoons extra virgin olive oil
Sea salt and freshly ground black pepper

1 cup crumbled feta cheese
½ red onion, thinly sliced
½ cup chopped fresh cilantro

Preheat the broiler or grill to high heat. If grilling, brush the grill surface with vegetable oil to prevent sticking.

Cut the watermelon into large squares, remove the rind, and broil or grill each piece for about 1 minute on each side. Remove from the heat and chill for 10 minutes.

Meanwhile, in a bowl, combine the yuzu juice and oil and add salt and pepper to taste. Add the watermelon, feta, onion, and cilantro. Toss to combine. Serve immediately.

PERFECTLY ROASTED
WILD MUSHROOMS (SERVES 4)

I love sitting down to a great steak and this side dish. You can serve it with anything, but it's even better when you put a spoonful on top of a nicely done cut of meat—don't forget the baked potato!

Technically, wild mushrooms include shiitakes, morels, chanterelles, oyster mushrooms, and puffballs, plus a few others. Button, cremini, and portobello mushrooms are cultivated. Most supermarkets carry a variety of wild mushrooms these days.

2 tablespoons extra virgin olive oil

1 pound mixed wild mushrooms, such as shiitake, oyster, and chanterelle

2 teaspoons sea salt

2 teaspoons freshly ground black pepper

2 tablespoons unsalted butter

1 bunch fresh thyme, leaves chopped

1 garlic clove, sliced

Heat the oil in a large skillet over high heat until it begins to smoke. Add the mushrooms and cook, stirring, until their water is released, 5 to 8 minutes. Add 1 teaspoon of the salt and 1 teaspoon pepper and cook, stirring occasionally, until the mushrooms are nicely browned, about 10 minutes more.

Add the butter, thyme, and garlic and stir until coated. Continue cooking for 5 minutes more, and season with the remaining salt and pepper. Serve immediately.

THE GAME CHANGERS—BURGERS! 4

FARMHOUSE BURGER

FARMHOUSE BACON CHEESEBURGER

SPIKE'S SUNNY-SIDE BURGER

GOOD STUFF MELT

COLLETTI'S SMOKEHOUSE BURGER

FREE-RANGE TURKEY BURGER

BREADED EGGPLANT, ROASTED PEPPER, GOAT CHEESE, AND ARUGULA'WICH

BLAZIN' BARN

UNCLE D'S CHILI AND CHEDDAR BURGER

VEGETARIANS ARE PEOPLE TOO

'SHROOM BURGER

PREZ OBAMA BURGER

SOUTHWESTERN BURGER

TAMARIND-GLAZED PORK BURGER WITH RED CABBAGE SLAW AND GRILLED PINEAPPLE

PORK AND PANCETTA BURGER WITH SMOKED MOZZARELLA, PEPERONATA, AND BASIL PESTO

FRIED CHICKEN BURGER WITH SMOKED BACON, GINGERED HONEY MUSTARD, AND SAUTÉED COLLARD GREENS

LAMB BURGER

CAPRESE BURGER

DOUBLE-ALE FISH BURGER

ROASTED CHICKEN WITH ROSEMARY AND HONEY MUSTARD GLAZE

MICHELLE'S MELT

STACKED WITH THE GOOD STUF

REDSKINS #74 SPICY CAJUN BURGER

HORTON'S KIDS GRILLED CHEESE

What can I say—devising the most **delicious** burger has pretty much changed my life! I've worked relentlessly on perfecting the recipe technically and **texturally**, and taste-fully! I've tried to build a **burger** for everyone, from the cowboy to the frat boy to the health nut to the First Lady in all women. Don't forget—toast them buns!

BURGER COOKING DONENESS

HEAT A LARGE SKILLET OVER MEDIUM HEAT AND PLACE PATTIES INTO THE SKILLET. COOK FOR:

1½ MINUTES ON EACH SIDE TO SEAR

2½ MINUTES ON EACH SIDE FOR RARE DONENESS

3 MINUTES ON EACH SIDE FOR MEDIUM-RARE DONENESS

4 MINUTES ON EACH SIDE FOR MEDIUM DONENESS

DON'T PRESS
DOWN ON
THE PATTIES!

THE TOASTING STATION

You cannot eat hamburgers without toasted buns. Not only does toasting add flavor to your burger, but it only takes a minute or two to get the bun perfectly brown—worth the extra step.

BEFORE YOU
DO ANYTHING

Before you do anything, precut 12-inch square pieces of wax paper, one for each burger. It's the secret to our success, and I share it with you below!

If you're grilling, toast the buns just before the burgers are done: Spread a little butter on cut surfaces of the buns, then put them face down on the top rack. Close the lid and a minute or two later, the buns are toasted and ready for toppings.

If you're not grilling, you can easily toast the buns under the broiler: Place the buns face up on a cookie sheet, put a dab of butter on them and broil for a few seconds—yes, seconds.

Once the buns are toasted, place the patty, lettuce, tomato, and onion over. Finish with a little sauce on the bun top.

This next step is the most important, and harks back to my grandfather's style of burger making. Take one precut sheet of wax paper, wrap the burger, and let it sit for 2 to 3 minutes. This will allow the buns to absorb the flavors of the meat and toppings.

IT'S WORTH THE EXTRA STEP

"CLASSICS, BUT WITH THE FLAVOR JUST BURSTING."

FARMHOUSE
BURGER (SERVES 6)

Who doesn't like these old-school basic recipes? They are among my favorites—classics but with the flavor just oozing from them. My grandfather always used to make the Farmhouse Cheeseburger because it's unheard-of to eat a burger without cheese in our house.

30 ounces ground sirloin
6 potato buns, cut in half
   Canola oil
   Sea salt and freshly
     ground black pepper
6 leaves iceberg lettuce

6 ruby-red tomato slices
6 red onion slices
12 pickle slices
   About 1 cup Good Stuff
    Sauce (page 35)

To make the patties, roll six 5-ounce sirloin balls and form each ball into a patty. Arrange on a tray, cover, and refrigerate.

Heat a large skillet over medium-high heat and add just enough oil to cover the entire bottom. When the oil begins to smoke, reduce the heat to medium and place the patties into the skillet. Season the patties with salt and pepper and cook for 3 minutes. Flip, and cook on the other side for 3 minutes more for medium-rare doneness.

Toast the buns according to directions on page 123. Set aside.

To assemble the burgers, place 1 patty on 1 toasted bun bottom. Top the patty with 1 lettuce leaf, 1 tomato slice, 1 onion slice, and 2 pickle slices. Dress with some of the sauce. Cover with the bun top. Repeat with the remaining ingredients. Don't forget to wrap the burgers in wax paper (page 123). Let rest for 2 to 3 minutes and serve.

FARMHOUSE CHEESEBURGER

Make the Farmhouse Burgers as described above, but place a slice of American cheese on top of each patty 2 minutes before they're done. Cover the pan with a lid for the last 30 seconds to melt the cheese.

FARMHOUSE BACON
CHEESEBURGER (SERVES 6)

What can make the All-American burger better? Its simple—add cheese, add bacon.

- 30 ounces ground sirloin
- 6 potato buns, cut in half
  Canola oil
- 1 pound applewood-
  smoked bacon
  Sea salt and freshly
  ground black pepper
- 6 slices American cheese
- 6 leaves iceberg lettuce
- 6 ruby red tomato slices
- 6 red onion slices
- 12 pickle slices
  About 1 cup Good Stuff
  Sauce (page 35)

To make the patties, roll six 5-ounce sirloin balls, and form each ball into a patty. Arrange on a tray, cover, and refrigerate. Line a plate with paper towels.

Heat a large skillet over medium-high heat, and add just enough oil to cover the entire bottom. When the oil begins to smoke, add the bacon and cook until crisp. Remove with a slotted spoon. Drain on the paper towels. Drain off the fat from the skillet but do not wipe clean.

Reduce the heat to medium and place the patties into the same skillet. Season the patties with salt and pepper and cook for 3 minutes. Flip, and cook on the other side for 1 minute. Place 3 strips of bacon and 1 slice of the cheese on each patty and continue to cook 2 minutes more for medium-rare doneness. Cover with a lid for the last 30 seconds to melt the cheese.

Toast the buns according to directions on page 123. Set aside.

To assemble the burgers, place 1 patty on 1 toasted bun bottom. Top the patty with 1 lettuce leaf, 1 tomato slice, 1 onion slice, and 2 pickle slices. Dress with some of the sauce. Cover with the bun top. Repeat with the remaining ingredients. Don't forget to wrap the sandwiches in wax paper (page 123). Let rest for 2 to 3 minutes and serve.

BIG STUFF BACON MELTDOWN
Double the amount of ground sirloin, make double the number of burgers, and layer two patties in each sandwich.

SPIKE'S SUNNY-SIDE BURGER (SERVES 6)

This mind-blowing burger (if I do say so myself) is derived from one of my favorite classic French dishes called croque madame, which is a sandwich of toasted ham, Gruyère cheese, and fried egg, topped with a béchamel sauce on a brioche bun. I knew there was a way to encapsulate these ingredients in a burger recipe, so I started playing around and voilà: My favorite burger was born. By the way, this baby is a hangover miracle, not that I condone such behavior.

30 ounces ground sirloin
6 brioche buns, cut in half
½ cup olive oil
6 large eggs
  Canola oil
1 pound applewood-smoked bacon

Salt and freshly ground black pepper
6 slices American cheese
6 leaves iceberg lettuce
6 ruby red tomato slices
6 red onion slices
12 pickle slices

About 1 cup Good Stuff Sauce (page 35)

To make the patties, roll six 5-ounce sirloin balls and form each ball into a patty. Arrange on a tray, cover, and refrigerate.

Heat the olive oil in a large nonstick skillet over medium heat. Line a plate with paper towels. Crack the eggs into the skillet, cover, and fry for 2 minutes. Remove with a slotted spoon. Drain on the paper towels. Discard the oil, or reserve it for another use if you'd like.

Reheat the skillet over medium-high heat and add just enough canola oil to cover the entire bottom. Line another plate with paper towels. Cook the bacon until crisp. Remove with a slotted spoon and drain on the paper towels. Drain off the fat from the skillet but do not wipe clean.

Reduce the heat to medium and place the patties into the same skillet. Season with salt and pepper and cook for 3 minutes. Flip, and cook on the other side for 1 minute. Place an equal amount of the bacon, 1 fried egg, and 1 slice of cheese on each patty and continue to cook 2 minutes more for medium-rare doneness. Cover with a lid for the last 30 seconds to melt the cheese.

Toast the buns according to directions on page 123. Set aside.

To assemble the burgers, place 1 patty on 1 toasted bun bottom. Top the patty with 1 lettuce leaf, 1 tomato slice, 1 onion slice, and 2 pickle slices. Dress with some of the sauce. Cover with the bun top. Repeat with the remaining ingredients. Don't forget to wrap the sandwiches in wax paper (page 123). Let rest for 2 to 3 minutes and serve.

GOOD STUFF
MELT (SERVES 4)

I'm a big fan of the patty melt—you can't really go wrong with caramelized onions and melted cheese. In fact, I could live off cheese on bread. Man, now I'm having flashbacks of living in Reims, France, breaking my back as an apprentice for Gérard Boyer! I think that's pretty much all I ate, but I worked at a chateau so I had to take a step up—caramelized onions, mushrooms, and two cheeses. It was divine. My point is, throw a burger in the mix and not just the cheddar, but your heart, too, will melt.

30 ounces ground sirloin	6 slices cheddar cheese	Salt and freshly ground
6 potato buns	1 recipe Perfectly Roasted	black pepper
¼ cup canola oil	Wild Mushrooms (page	
2 cups thinly sliced	115)	
Spanish onions	About 1 cup Good Stuff	
6 slices Muenster cheese	Sauce (page 35)	

To make the patties, roll four 5½-ounce sirloin balls and form each ball into a patty. Arrange on a tray, cover, and refrigerate.

To make caramelized onions, heat the oil in a large nonstick skillet over medium heat. Add the onions—don't worry if they're piled high; they will cook down. Turn with a spatula so all the onions are evenly coated in oil. Continue to cook, turning the onions every 8 minutes, until the slices have turned a dark, rich brown color, about 25 minutes. If the onions begin to burn, reduce the heat to medium-low and add more oil. Remove the onions and place them in a bowl.

Increase the heat to medium (if you had to reduce it) and place the patties into the skillet. Season the patties with salt and pepper and cook for 3 minutes. Flip, and cook on the other side for 1 minute. Place 1 slice each of the two cheeses, some of the mushrooms, and some of the caramelized onions on each patty and continue to cook 2 minutes more for medium-rare doneness. Cover with a lid for the last 30 seconds to melt the cheese.

Toast the buns according to directions on page 123. Set aside.

To assemble the burgers, place 1 patty on 1 toasted bun bottom. Dress with some of the sauce. Cover with the bun top. Repeat with the remaining ingredients. Don't forget to wrap the sandwiches in wax paper (page 123). Let rest for 2 to 3 minutes and serve.

COLLETTI'S SMOKEHOUSE BURGER (SERVES 6)

Colletti. You can't really describe him at all, Michael Jesepi Colletti, a guy I met and helped open Le Cirque in New York City. He's *The Sopranos* meets an oversized teddy bear meets a chef, all rolled into a New Jersey guy with a nice gold chain, baggy jeans, and a rapper walk. His is the burger Good Stuff Eatery sells the most and it still kinda kills me that this one wins over Spike's Sunny-Side Burger (page 128). But I thought it better not to fudge the numbers, and I give credit where it's due.

CHIPOTLE-BARBECUE SAUCE (Makes 3 cups)
- Half a 7-ounce can chipotle chiles in adobo sauce
- 2 cups sweet, mild barbecue sauce
- ½ cup ketchup
- ¼ cup apple cider vinegar
- 1 tablespoon molasses

BURGERS
- 30 ounces ground sirloin
- 6 potato buns, cut in half
- Canola oil
- 1 pound applewood-smoked bacon
- Sea salt and freshly ground black pepper
- 6 slices cheddar cheese
- 1½ cups Chipotle-Barbecue Sauce
- 1 recipe Cliff's Homegrown Vidalia Onion Petals (page 81)

To make the Chipotle-Barbecue Sauce, add the chipotles to a food processor or blender. Puree until smooth. Add the barbecue sauce, ketchup, vinegar, and molasses. Puree until smooth. Strain the mixture through a fine-mesh strainer to remove the seeds. Set aside until ready to use.

To make the patties, roll six 5-ounce sirloin balls and form each ball into a patty. Arrange on a tray, cover, and refrigerate.

Heat a large skillet over medium-high heat and add just enough oil to cover the entire bottom. Line a plate with paper towels. When the oil begins to smoke, add the bacon and cook until crisp. Remove with a slotted spoon. Drain on the paper towels. Drain off the fat from the skillet but do not wipe clean.

Reduce the heat to medium and place the patties into the skillet. Season the patties with salt and pepper and cook for 3 minutes. Flip, and cook for 1 minute. Place an equal amount of bacon and 1 slice cheese on each patty and continue to cook 2 minutes more for medium-rare doneness. Cover with a lid for the last 30 seconds to melt the cheese.

Toast the buns according to directions on page 123. Set aside.

To assemble the burgers, place 1 patty on 1 toasted bun bottom. Top the patty with some of the sauce and onion petals. Cover with the bun top. Repeat with the remaining ingredients. Don't forget to wrap the sandwiches in wax paper (page 123). Let rest for 2 to 3 minutes and serve.

FREE-RANGE TURKEY BURGER (SERVES 6)

I will admit to studying my share of women. I mean I am a young, fun chef—how can I not? While I don't understand most of them, one thing has become perfectly clear—the ladies love turkey burgers. They think traditional burgers result in hours at the gym (not necessarily the case), so they turn to the leaner, less-threatening alternative—turkey. Now, when it comes to women, I aim to please. This turkey burger is so good, it's almost better than the real thing. And as long as I'm not in the doghouse for this confession, I might even have one for lunch. For a variation, try topping this burger with the Cranberry Sauce recipe that follows instead of the Chunky Avocado Topping.

TURKEY MIX
- 2 tablespoons butter
- 1 cup diced celery
- 1 cup diced scallions
- 2 green apples, diced
- ½ cup canned chipotle chiles in adobo sauce
- 1 cup Major Grey's Chutney
- 30 ounces ground turkey
- ½ cup freshly grated lemon zest
- ½ cup fresh lemon juice
- 1 teaspoon sea salt
- 1 teaspoon freshly ground black pepper

CHUNKY AVOCADO TOPPING
- 3 large avocados, pit and peel removed and diced
- 1 cup chopped fresh cilantro
- ½ red onion, diced
- Grated zest and juice of 2 lemons
- 2 teaspoons olive oil
- Salt

BURGERS
- 6 multigrain potato buns, cut in half
- Canola oil
- Sea salt and freshly ground black pepper
- 6 slices Muenster cheese
- 6 leaves iceberg lettuce
- 6 ruby red tomato slices
- 6 red onion slices

To make the turkey mixture, melt the butter in a skillet over medium heat. Add the celery, scallions, and apples and cook, stirring, for 15 to 20 minutes. Remove from the heat and set aside. Put the chipotle peppers and chutney in a blender. Puree until smooth. Transfer to a bowl with the turkey, celery mixture, lemon zest, and lemon juice and combine well. Set aside until ready to use.

To make the topping, in a bowl, combine the avocado, cilantro, onion, lemon zest and juice, olive oil, and salt to taste and mash together until well blended. Set aside until ready to use.

To make the patties, roll six 5-ounce turkey balls and form each ball into a patty. Arrange on a tray, cover, and refrigerate.

Toast the buns according to directions on page 123. Set aside.

Heat a large skillet over medium-high heat and add just enough oil to cover the entire bottom. After 2 minutes, reduce the heat to medium, and place the patties into the skillet. Season the patties with salt and pepper and cook for 3 minutes. Flip, and cook on the other side for 1 minute. Place 1 slice cheese on each patty and continue to cook 2 minutes more for medium-rare doneness. Cover with a lid for the last 30 seconds to melt the cheese.

To assemble the burgers, place 1 patty on 1 toasted bun bottom. Top the patty with 1 lettuce leaf, 1 tomato slice, 1 onion slice, and a spoonful of the avocado topping. Cover with the bun top. Repeat with the remaining ingredients. Don't forget to wrap the sandwiches in wax paper (page 123). Let rest for 2 to 3 minutes and serve.

CRANBERRY
SAUCE (MAKES ABOUT 4 CUPS)

This goes great on a turkey burger. Try it in place of the Chunky Avocado Topping in the preceding recipe. Bruising the ginger releases its juices, and that enhances its potency and flavor.

1 **1-inch piece fresh ginger**
2 **cups fresh or frozen
    cranberries**
1 **cup sugar**
1 **cup fresh orange juice
    Salt**

Put the ginger on a flat surface and hit it with the broad side of a cleaver or large knife. Place all the ingredients into a large saucepan, and cook over medium heat, stirring, until the sugar dissolves and the liquid comes to a boil. Reduce the heat to low and continue to cook and stir until the mixture thickens, about 20 minutes. Remove from the heat, discard the ginger, and cool the sauce. The sauce can be refrigerated in an airtight container for up to 1 week.

BREADED EGGPLANT, ROASTED PEPPER, GOAT CHEESE, AND ARUGULA 'WICH (SERVES 6)

For vegetarians this is a delicious alternative to the meatier recipes. And don't be fooled, ya carnivore bullies, this 'wich is fit for a king.

1 cup extra virgin olive oil
1 tablespoon chopped fresh oregano
1 tablespoon chopped fresh basil
1 clove garlic, chopped Salt and freshly ground black pepper

2 eggplants, cut into three 1-inch-thick slices
2 red bell peppers, sliced
2 cups all-purpose flour
5 large eggs, well beaten
2 cups seasoned breadcrumbs
6 potato buns, cut in half

1 cup Balsamic Mayonnaise (page 41)
1 4-ounce log goat cheese, cut into ½-inch rounds
½ pound baby arugula

In a large bowl, combine ¾ cup of the oil, the oregano, basil, garlic, and salt and pepper to taste. Add the eggplant. Coat all sides. Refrigerate for 1 hour.

Meanwhile, place the bell peppers directly on your gas stove-top burner until charred on all sides, turning frequently. Alternatively, place the red peppers on a baking sheet, and broil for 5 minutes, turning till all sides are charred. Place the peppers in a paper bag until cool enough to handle, about 10 minutes. Peel the peppers (the blackened skin should scrape off easily) and discard the seeds. Set aside until ready to use.

Remove the eggplant slices from the marinade and pat dry. Put the flour into one wide-mouthed bowl, the eggs in a second bowl, and the breadcrumbs in a third. Dip each eggplant slice into the flour, then the eggs, and then the breadcrumbs. Set aside.

Heat the remaining ¼ cup oil in a large skillet over medium heat. Line a plate with paper towels. When the oil is hot, add the eggplant and fry until golden on both sides, 3 minutes each side. Drain on the paper towels.

Toast the buns according to directions on page 123.

To assemble the burgers, spread some of the mayonnaise on 1 toasted bun top. Place 1 eggplant slice on the bottom of the bun. Top with some roasted peppers, a goat cheese slice, and some arugula. Cover with the bun top. Repeat with the remaining ingredients. Don't forget to wrap the sandwiches in wax paper (page 123). Let rest for 2 to 3 minutes and serve.

BLAZIN' BARN (SERVES 6)

The first time I ever tasted a bahn mi sandwich was on Mulberry Street in New York's Vietnamese neighborhood. It had thinly sliced pickled carrots and daikon, onions, cucumbers, cilantro, jalapeño peppers, roasted pork, Vietnamese ham, paté, mayonnaise, and head cheese. I thought it was the best thing I'd ever tasted. The ingredients danced in your mouth. So, of course, I had to figure out how to make a burger with those flavors. I think we came pretty close.

PICKLED CARROTS AND DAIKON
- 2 large carrots, peeled and julienned
- 1 large daikon, peeled and julienned
- 2 cups white vinegar
- 2 cups sugar

BURGERS
- 30 ounces ground sirloin
- 6 potato buns, cut in half
- Canola oil
- Sea salt and freshly ground black pepper
- ¼ cup chopped fresh basil
- ¼ cup chopped fresh cilantro

- 1 cup Sriracha Mayonnaise (page 38)

To pickle the carrots and daikon, put each of them into two separate bowls. Add the vinegar, sugar, and ½ cup water to a large saucepan over medium heat. Bring to a boil. Pour evenly over the carrots and daikon and cool to room temperature for 30 minutes. Refrigerate until ready to use, up to 1 week if covered—they will become more flavorful over time.

To make the patties, roll six 5-ounce sirloin balls and form each ball into a patty. Arrange on a tray, cover, and refrigerate.

Toast the buns according to directions on page 123. Set aside.

Heat a large skillet over medium-high heat and add just enough oil to cover the entire bottom. When the oil begins to smoke, reduce the heat to medium and place the patties into the skillet. Season the patties with salt and pepper, and cook for 3 minutes. Flip, and cook on the other side 3 minutes more for medium-rare doneness.

To assemble the burgers, mix together the basil and cilantro. Place 1 patty on 1 toasted bun bottom. Top the patty with some of each of the pickled carrots, daikon, and the basil-cilantro mix. Spread some of the mayonnaise on the bun top and cover. Repeat with the remaining ingredients. Don't forget to wrap the sandwiches in wax paper (page 123). Let rest for 2 to 3 minutes and serve.

UNCLE D'S CHILI AND CHEDDAR BURGER (SERVES 6)

My great-uncle Denny was the type of guy who was full of shtick. You can't find any more people like him around. He was that old-school funnyman, the comedian and prankster in the family; he and my grandfather were best friends. In 1944, my grandfather was 18 years old and he was working as a soda jerk in his father's restaurant, Paul's Sandwich Shop, in Montreal, Canada.

So the story goes, my grandfather had his back to the counter and all he heard was "I want a Coke float with a big lump of sugar in it for my horse." When he turned around, his friend and later-to-be brother-in-law, Denny, was sitting sidesaddle on a horse. Chaos ensued in the restaurant but Uncle Denny and my grandfather were left to it, howling hysterically. So here's to you, Uncle D—thanks for all the laughs!

30 ounces ground sirloin
6 potato buns, cut in half
  Canola oil
  Salt and freshly ground
  black pepper

1 recipe Uncle D's Chili (page 84)
1 recipe Cheddar Cheese Sauce (page 87)
1½ cups sour cream

1½ cups sliced scallions

To make the patties, roll six 5-ounce sirloin balls and form each ball into a patty. Arrange on a tray, cover, and refrigerate.

Toast the buns according to directions on page 123. Set aside.

Heat a large skillet over medium-high heat and add just enough oil to cover the entire bottom. When the oil begins to smoke, reduce the heat to medium and place the patties into the skillet. Season the patties with salt and pepper and cook for 3 minutes. Flip, and cook on the other side for 3 minutes more for medium-rare doneness.

To assemble the burgers, place 1 patty on 1 toasted bun bottom. Top the patty with some chili and cheese sauce, ¼ cup sour cream, and ¼ cup scallions. Cover with the bun top. Repeat with the remaining ingredients. Don't forget to wrap the sandwiches in wax paper (page 123). Let rest for 2 to 3 minutes and serve.

VEGETARIANS ARE PEOPLE TOO
'SHROOM BURGER (SERVES 6)

This one is owed to Billy Ivey and Ted McCoig because I loved the way they named it, and we love them because they, our branding guys for Good Stuff Eatery, gave the place its vibe. This is a shout-out to those who want to come in and don't want to eat a salad. We love you too.

- 12 3- to 4-inch diameter portobello mushrooms, stems removed
- 6 potato buns, cut in half
- 2 tablespoons olive oil
- 2 tablespoons chopped fresh thyme
- 1 tablespoon sea salt, plus more for sprinkling
- 1½ teaspoons freshly ground black pepper, plus more for sprinkling
- 12 slices cheddar cheese
- 12 slices Muenster cheese
- 2 cups all-purpose flour
- 8 large eggs, well beaten
- ½ cup panko breadcrumbs
- 6 cups canola oil
- 6 leaves iceberg lettuce
- 6 slices ruby red tomato
- 1 red onion, thinly sliced
- 1 pickle, cut into rounds
- ¼ cup Good Stuff Sauce (page 35)

Preheat the oven to 400°F. Place the mushrooms, stem side up, in a roasting pan and roast for 20 minutes, or until soft. Remove from the oven and let cool. Lower the oven temperature to 350°F.

Toast the buns according to directions on page 123. Set aside.

In a medium bowl, combine the olive oil, thyme, salt, and pepper and stir to mix well. Coat the mushrooms. Take 1 mushroom, layer 2 slices of each cheese on top, and place another mushroom on top to make a sandwich.

Put the flour into one wide-mouthed bowl, the eggs in a second bowl, and the breadcrumbs in a third. Dip each mushroom "sandwich" into the flour, then the eggs, and then the breadcrumbs. Set aside.

Heat the canola oil in a large ovenproof skillet over medium heat. Line a platter with paper towels.

When the oil is hot, add the mushrooms and cook till golden brown on each side, about 2 minutes on each side. Transfer the skillet to the oven and bake for 5 minutes. Remove the mushrooms with a slotted spoon. Drain on the paper towels. Sprinkle with salt and pepper.

To assemble the burgers, place 1 mushroom patty on 1 toasted bun bottom. Top the patty with 1 lettuce leaf, 1 tomato slice, a few onion slices, and a few pickle slices. Spread 1 tablespoon sauce on the top bun and cover. Repeat with the remaining ingredients. Don't forget to wrap the sandwiches in wax paper (page 123). Let rest for 2 to 3 minutes and serve.

SOME
BURGERS
ARE
SHOW-OFFS

PREZ OBAMA BURGER (SERVES 6)

The 2008 presidential election happened the year I moved to D.C. Because I had a restaurant on Capitol Hill, how could I not do a McCain vs. Obama Burger! What I didn't realize is how seriously people would take this "Countdown to Election" burger challenge. I think bipartisan couples were getting divorced in front of my cashiers, first-time dates were finding out way too much information, and there were a few wacky but lovable Democrats coming in to order the Obama burger (so it would count toward the vote) but who wanted all the McCain ingredients. Not only did Obama win in my burger competition by four to one (which I'm sure he was worried about) but he also won the big one—44th President of the United States. So "Yes We Did" put it on the menu as the Prez Obama Burger. Here's what I thought a cool Chicago guy would like on his burger—hopefully I'm right.

HORSERADISH MAYONNAISE (Makes about 2½ cups)
- 2 cups Homemade Basic Mayonnaise (page 34)
- 4 ounces prepared horseradish
- 1 tablespoon cayenne
- 1½ teaspoon freshly ground black pepper
- Sea salt

RED ONION MARMALADE
- 2 red onions
- 1 cup red wine vinegar
- 1 cup sugar

BURGERS
- 30 ounces ground sirloin
- 6 potato buns, cut in half
- Canola oil
- 1 pound applewood-smoked bacon
- Sea salt and freshly ground black pepper
- 1 pound crumbled blue cheese

To make the Horseradish Mayonnaise, add the basic mayonnaise, horseradish, cayenne, pepper, and salt to taste to a food processor or blender. Puree until smooth. The mayonnaise can be refrigerated in an airtight container for up to 1 week.

To make the Red Onion Marmalade, slice both red onions ½ inch thick. Add the vinegar and sugar to a pot over medium heat. Bring to a simmer. Once the sugar is completely dissolved, add the onions. Cook, stirring constantly to prevent burning, until the onions are translucent and the liquid is reduced by half, about 5 minutes. Set aside to cool.

To make the patties, roll six 5-ounce sirloin balls and form each ball into a patty. Arrange on a tray, cover, and refrigerate.

Toast the buns according to directions on page 123. Set aside.

Heat a large skillet over medium-high heat and just add enough oil to cover the entire bottom. Line a plate with paper towels. When the oil begins to smoke, add the bacon and cook until crisp. Remove with a slotted spoon. Drain on the paper towels. Drain the fat from the pan but do not wipe clean.

Reduce the heat to medium and place the patties into the skillet. Season the patties with salt and pepper and cook for 3 minutes. Flip, and cook on the other side for 1 minute more. Distribute the crumbled blue cheese equally among the patties and continue to cook 2 minutes more for medium-rare doneness. Cover with a lid for the last 30 seconds to melt the cheese.

To assemble the burgers, place 1 patty on 1 bun bottom. Top the patty with some mayonnaise, marmalade, and bacon. Cover with the bun top. Repeat with the remaining ingredients. Don't forget to wrap the sandwiches in wax paper (page 123). Let rest for 2 to 3 minutes and serve.

SOUTHWESTERN
BURGER (SERVES 6)

Every once in a while I can scarf down some super-spicy food. This has the best of everything: a spicy cheese, hot mayo, and a tasty salsa with a kick. It will set your mouth on fire, but it's totally worth it.

30 ounces ground sirloin
 6 potato buns, cut in half
   Canola oil
   Salt and freshly ground
     black pepper

 6 slices Monterey Jack
     cheese
 1 recipe Roasted Corn
     and Red Pepper Salsa
     (page 104)

 1 cup Chipotle Mayonnaise
     (page 36)

To make the patties, roll six 5-ounce sirloin balls and form each ball into a patty. Arrange on a tray, cover, and refrigerate.

Toast the buns according to directions on page 123. Set aside.

Heat a large skillet over medium-high heat and add just enough oil to cover the entire bottom. When the oil begins to smoke, reduce the heat to medium, and place the patties into the skillet. Season the patties with salt and pepper, and cook for 3 minutes. Flip, and cook on the other side for 1 minute more. Place 1 slice cheese on each patty and continue cooking 2 minutes more for medium-rare doneness. Cover with a lid for the last 30 seconds to melt the cheese.

To assemble the burgers, place 1 patty on 1 toasted bun bottom. Spoon some salsa on each patty. Spread some of the mayonnaise on the bun top and cover. Repeat with the remaining ingredients. Don't forget to wrap the sandwiches in wax paper (page 123). Let rest for 2 to 3 minutes and serve.

TAMARIND-GLAZED PORK BURGER WITH RED CABBAGE SLAW AND GRILLED PINEAPPLE (SERVES 6)

Nothing gets my palate inspired more than the flavors of Vietnam—sweet, salty, sour. Can't. Get. Enough. Traveling throughout Vietnam you see grilled pineapples everywhere and I thought pairing it with the tamarind pulp would make a great combo. Tamarind pulp is packaged and sold in cellophane-wrapped blocks in most Asian markets. You can find already prepared tamarind liquid, but it won't have the same flavor.

TAMARIND GLAZE
- ½ cup (6 ounces) tamarind pulp with seeds
- ½ cup boiling water
- ¾ cup honey
- ¼ cup Thai fish sauce
- 2 Thai chiles, minced
- 2 garlic cloves, minced
  Sea salt

ASIAN PORK BURGERS
- 2 tablespoons canola oil plus more for cooking
- ½ red onion, chopped
- 1 garlic clove, chopped
- 30 ounces ground pork
- 2 Thai chiles, chopped
- ¼ cup dark brown sugar
- 2 tablespoons freshly ground black pepper
- 2 tablespoons Thai fish sauce
- 1 tablespoon sea salt, plus more for sprinkling
- 6 potato buns, cut in half
- ½ pineapple, cored and sliced into six ¼-inch-thick slices
- 1 cup Red Cabbage Slaw (page 99)

To make the glaze, in a medium bowl, combine the tamarind and boiling water, stirring to separate the pulp from the seeds. Strain through a coarse-mesh strainer, pressing with a rubber spatula to extract all of the liquid and remove the seeds and fibers. Stir in the honey, fish sauce, chiles, and garlic, and season with salt. Divide the glaze into two batches; one will be for grilling and one for topping the burgers. Set aside until ready to use.

To make the burgers, heat the 2 tablespoons oil in a large skillet over medium heat. When the oil is smoking, add the onion and cook, stirring, until lightly brown, about 3 minutes. Add the garlic and cook, stirring, for 2 minutes more. Remove and set aside to cool.

In a large bowl, combine the ground pork, the onion-garlic mixture, the chiles, sugar, pepper, fish sauce, and salt and mix very well. To make the patties, roll six 5-ounce pork balls and form each ball into a patty. Arrange on a tray, cover, and refrigerate.

Toast the buns according to directions on page 123. Set aside.

Preheat a grill or griddle and brush with oil. Alternatively, heat a large skillet over medium heat and brush with oil. Brush the pineapple slices with oil, sprinkle with salt, place on the grill, and cook until caramelized on both sides. Add the burgers to the grill and brush from one of the batches of glaze, and cook for 5 to 7 minutes. Flip the burgers, brush with the glaze again, and cook for 5 to 7 minutes more. (Alternatively you may cook the burgers in the large skillet over medium-high heat.)

To assemble the burgers, brush 1 toasted bun bottom and top with some of the unused batch of glaze (do not use the batch you used for brushing the raw patties). Place 1 patty on the bun bottom and top with 1 slice pineapple and 1 spoonful slaw. Cover with the bun top. Repeat with remaining ingredients. Don't forget to wrap the sandwiches in wax paper (page 123). Let rest for 2 to 3 minutes and serve.

PORK AND PANCETTA BURGER WITH SMOKED MOZZARELLA, PEPERONATA, AND BASIL PESTO
(SERVES 6)

With a name like Mendelsohn, you might not imagine me pining for pork. Wrong! I'm absolutely infatuated with the other white meat, which is why this burger steals my heart.

- 1 tablespoon plus 2 teaspoons olive oil
- ½ cup diced Spanish onion
- 1 clove garlic, minced
- 25 ounces ground pork
- 5 ounces ground pancetta
- 1 teaspoon chopped fresh rosemary
- 1 teaspoon sea salt, plus more for sprinkling
- 1 teaspoon freshly ground black pepper, plus more for sprinkling
- ½ teaspoon crushed red pepper
- 6 focaccia rolls, cut in half
- 1 cup Peperonata (page 105)
- 6 slices smoked mozzarella
- 1 cup Basil Pesto (page 154)

Heat the 1 tablespoon oil in a large skillet over medium heat. When the oil is smoking, add the onion and cook, stirring, until lightly brown, about 2 minutes. Add the garlic and cook, stirring, for 2 minutes more. Remove and set aside to cool.

In a bowl, combine the pork, pancetta, the onion-garlic mixture, the rosemary, salt, pepper, crushed red pepper, and the remaining 2 teaspoons oil and mix very well. To make the patties, roll six 5-ounce pork-pancetta balls and form each ball into a patty. Arrange on a tray, cover, and refrigerate.

Toast the rolls according to directions on page 123. Set aside. Heat the Peperonata.

Heat a large skillet over medium-high heat and add just enough oil to cover the entire bottom. When the oil begins to smoke, reduce the heat to medium and place the patties into the skillet. Season the patties with salt and pepper and cook for 5 minutes. Flip, and cook on the other side for another 1 minute. Place 1 slice cheese on each patty and continue to cook 2 minutes more. Cover with a lid for the last 30 seconds to melt the cheese.

To assemble the burgers, spread some of the pesto on 1 toasted bun top and bottom. Place 1 patty on 1 bun bottom. Top with a spoonful of Peperonata, and *badda bing*. Cover with the bun top. Repeat with the remaining ingredients. Don't forget to wrap the sandwiches in wax paper (page 123). Let rest for 2 to 3 minutes and serve.

BASIL
PESTO (MAKES ABOUT 1 CUP)

½ cup packed fresh basil
   leaves
2 or 3 cloves garlic
¼ cup pine nuts
¼ cup extra virgin olive oil

Pinch crushed red
   pepper
Sea salt and freshly
   ground black pepper

Add the basil, garlic, pine nuts, olive oil, crushed red pepper, and salt and pepper to taste to a food processor or blender. Puree until smooth. This can be refrigerated in an airtight container for up to 1 week.

FRIED CHICKEN BURGER WITH SMOKED BACON, GINGERED HONEY MUSTARD, AND SAUTÉED COLLARD GREENS (SERVES 6)

Call me uncouth. Call me uncivilized. I don't care. I'm nuts about old-fashioned fried chicken from a big ol' bucket. Bring it on!!! We made it a bit more presentable by making this greasy goodness less greasy and jazzing it up inside a sandwich, but either way, it's finger-lickin' good.

You'll probably have extra Gingered Honey Mustard since you only need about a cup for this recipe. Use it as a great dip with veggies, or you can store it in an airtight container in the fridge for up to 2 weeks.

GINGERED HONEY MUSTARD (Makes about 2½ cups)
- 2 cups honey
- 1 1-inch piece fresh ginger
- ½ cup white wine vinegar
- 1 tablespoon Dijon mustard
- Pinch ground ginger

BURGERS
- 1 cup canola oil
- 1 large onion, chopped
- 30 ounces ground chicken breast
- 1 teaspoon cayenne
- 1 teaspoon paprika
- 1 teaspoon garlic salt
- 6 potato buns, cut in half
- 1 pound applewood-smoked bacon
- 2 garlic cloves, chopped
- 1 pound collard greens, chopped
- Sea salt and freshly ground black pepper
- 2 cups all-purpose flour
- 5 large eggs, lightly beaten
- 2 cups unseasoned breadcrumbs

To make the mustard, combine the honey and fresh ginger in a large saucepan over medium-low heat. Cook until the mixture reduces by half, about 20 minutes. Remove from the heat and cool. When cool, discard the ginger. Transfer to a food processor or blender. Add the vinegar, mustard, and ground ginger. Puree until smooth. Set aside until ready to use.

To make the burgers, heat 1 tablespoon of the oil in a large skillet over medium heat. Add the onion and cook, stirring occasionally, until lightly brown, about 3 minutes. Set aside to cool.

In a large bowl, combine the ground chicken, cayenne, paprika, garlic salt, and cooled onion and mix very well. To make the patties, roll six 5-ounce chicken balls and form each ball into a patty. Arrange on a tray, cover, and refrigerate.

Toast the buns according to directions on page 123. Set aside.

(CONTINUED ON PAGE 156)

FRIED CHICKEN BURGER WITH SMOKED BACON, GINGERED HONEY MUSTARD, AND SAUTÉED COLLARD GREENS (CONTINUED FROM PAGE 155)

Reheat the skillet over medium-high heat and add just enough of the remaining oil to cover the entire bottom. Line a plate with paper towels. When the oil begins to smoke, add the bacon and cook until crisp. Remove with a slotted spoon. Drain on the paper towels.

Add the garlic to the bacon drippings and cook, stirring, for about 5 minutes. Add the collard greens and salt and pepper to taste. Cover, and steam over medium heat until the greens wilt, about 20 minutes.

Put the flour into one bowl, the eggs in a second bowl, and the breadcrumbs in a third. Dip each chicken patty into the flour, then the eggs, and then the breadcrumbs. Set aside.

Heat the remaining oil in a second large skillet over medium-high heat. When the oil begins to smoke, reduce the heat to medium and place the patties into the skillet. Season the patties with salt and pepper and cook for 6 minutes. Flip, and cook on the other side for 6 minutes.

To assemble the burgers, spread some of the mustard on 1 toasted bun bottom and 1 top. Place 1 patty on the bun bottom. Top with a portion of collard greens and bacon. Cover with the bun top. Repeat with the remaining ingredients. Don't forget to wrap the sandwiches in wax paper (page 123). Let rest for 2 to 3 minutes and serve.

"IF YOU WANT TO SWITCH IT UP, JUST CLUCK IT!"

LAMB
BURGER (SERVES 6)

I've never met a lamb I didn't love. So how could I exclude my favorite protein from my favorite pasttime (burgers!)? I know what you're thinking: My Big Fat Greek Burger. *Opah*!

WHIPPED FETA
1 pound feta cheese (preferably Bulgarian), crumbled
⅓ cup chopped jalapeño peppers
¼ cup extra virgin olive oil
1 teaspoon freshly ground black pepper
2 tablespoons fresh lemon juice

CUMIN-SCENTED YOGURT
(Makes about 3 cups)
1 teaspoon ground cumin
2 cups plain Greek yogurt
½ cup fresh lemon juice
1 tablespoon honey
1½ teaspoons salt

LAMB BURGERS
½ pound arugula
⅓ cup extra virgin olive oil
¼ cup fresh lemon juice
32 ounces ground lamb
8 ounces ground pork
4 cloves garlic, roasted (see Note)
2 teaspoons Dijon mustard
2 teaspoons chopped fresh mint
2 teaspoons chopped fresh parsley
¼ cup chopped onion
2 teaspoons sea salt
2 teaspoons freshly ground black pepper
1 teaspoon dried oregano
Canola oil
6 sesame seed potato buns
6 ruby red tomato slices
1 small red onion, thinly sliced

To make the whipped cheese, place the feta, jalapeño peppers, oil, black pepper, and lemon juice in a food processor or blender. Pulse on and off until smooth and creamy, about 4 minutes. Set aside until ready to use.

To make the yogurt, toast the ground cumin in a dry skillet over low heat, stirring constantly to prevent burning, until fragrant, about 1 minute. Transfer to a food processor or blender. Add the yogurt, lemon juice, honey, and salt. Puree until smooth. Set aside until ready to use.

For the burgers, place the arugula in a bowl. In another bowl, mix together the olive oil and lemon juice. Toss with the arugula. Set aside until ready to use.

In another bowl, combine the lamb, pork, roasted garlic, mustard, mint, parsley, onion, salt, pepper, and oregano, and mix very well. To make the patties, roll six 5-ounce lamb-pork balls and form each ball into a patty. Arrange on a tray, cover, and refrigerate.

Toast the buns according to directions on page 123. Set aside.

Heat a large skillet over medium-high heat and add just enough oil to cover the entire bottom. When the skillet begins to smoke, reduce the heat to medium and place the patties into the skillet. Season the patties with salt and pepper and cook for 3 minutes. Flip, and cook on the other side for another 3 minutes for medium-rare doneness.

To assemble the burgers, place 1 patty on 1 toasted bun bottom. Top the patty with 1 tomato slice, a few onion slices, 2 tablespoons whipped cheese, and some arugula. Cover with the bun top. Repeat with the remaining ingredients. Don't forget to wrap the burger in wax paper (page 123). Let rest for 2 to 3 minutes and serve.

NOTE

To roast garlic: Preheat the oven to 400°F. Cut ½ inch off the top of the head of the garlic to expose the individual cloves of garlic. Place in a pie plate. Drizzle 2 teaspoons extra virgin olive oil and cover the pie plate tightly with foil. Bake for 30 minutes. Remove and let cool. When slightly cooled, release the skin around each clove with a paring knife and then squeeze the garlic out of the skins.

CAPRESE
BURGER (SERVES 6)

I've always loved Italian food. Pasta, fresh tomatoes, smelly cheeses, deep red wine, braised meats. I mean, almost every dish is the best thing you've ever tasted, if done right. Every once in a while I like to eat light, and I thought up this recipe after going to the market and buying these bright red fresh tomatoes and this smooth mozzarella cheese from a local farmer.

3 beefsteak tomatoes, cored and cut in half
½ cup extra virgin olive oil
  Sea salt and freshly ground black pepper
½ garlic clove, minced
6 basil leaves, julienned
6 potato buns, cut in half

1 pound fresh mozzarella, cut into 6 thick slices
3 tablespoons store-bought balsamic vinaigrette
½ cup Basil Pesto (page 154)

Preheat the oven to 300°F. Put the 6 tomato halves, flesh side up, on a baking sheet. Drizzle each with some of the olive oil, 1 teaspoon each of salt and pepper, some minced garlic, and some basil. Cook for 45 minutes to 1 hour or until tomatoes are soft when a fork is inserted.

Toast the buns according to directions on page 123. Set aside.

To assemble the burgers, place a tomato half on the bottom bun. Top with 1 mozzarella slice on the tomato, 1½ teaspoons vinaigrette, and season with salt and black pepper. Spread the pesto on the bun top and cover. Repeat with the remaining ingredients. Don't forget to wrap the burgers in wax paper (page 123). Let rest for 2 to 3 minutes and serve.

DOUBLE-ALE
FISH BURGER (SERVES 6)

The Brits might not be known for their food, but good fish 'n' chips is nothing short of brilliant. So in honor of my friends across the pond, here's a double-ale fried fish with Malted Caper Mayo that would make the Queen want to kiss me.

Store any extra mayonnaise in an airtight container in the fridge for up to 2 weeks.

MALTED CAPER MAYONNAISE (Makes about 2½ cups)
- 2 cups Homemade Basic Mayonnaise (page 34)
- 2 tablespoons chopped rinsed capers
- 1 tablespoon dark brown sugar
- 1½ teaspoons fresh lemon juice
- 1½ teaspoons malt vinegar
- Pinch salt
- Pinch cracked pink peppercorns or black pepper

BATTERED FISH
- 3 cups all-purpose flour
- 2 tablespoons baking powder
- 2 teaspoons sea salt
- ½ teaspoon cayenne
- 1 bottle pale ale
- 1 bottle dark ale
- 2 cups canola oil
- 2 cups cornstarch
- 2½ pounds cod fillets, cut into 1-ounce strips
- 6 potato buns, cut in half
- 6 leaves Bibb lettuce
- 2 tomatoes, sliced into thirds
- 1 lemon, cut in half
- 1 recipe Sunny's Hand-Cut Fries (page 71)
- 1 recipe Old Bay Mayonnaise (page 39)

To make the mayonnaise, add the Homemade Basic Mayonnaise, capers, brown sugar, lemon juice, vinegar, salt, and peppercorns to a food processor or blender. Puree until smooth. The mayonnaise can be refrigerated in an airtight container for up to 1 week.

To make the fish, in a bowl, whisk together the flour, baking powder, salt, and cayenne. Add the two beers into the dry ingredients, whisking to prevent any lumps. Refrigerate for 30 minutes.

Heat the oil in a large skillet over medium heat. Line a platter with paper towels. Meanwhile, put the cornstarch into one bowl. Dip each fish strip in the cornstarch to cover, then into the batter. Place the fish into the hot oil using a slotted spoon. Fry for about 4 minutes, then turn the strips over and cook until the strips turn a golden brown, about 4 minutes more. Remove with a slotted spoon. Drain on the paper towels.

Toast the buns according to directions on page 123. Set aside.

To assemble the burgers, divide the fish strips equally among the bun bottoms. Top with 1 lettuce leaf and 1 tomato slice. Squeeze some lemon juice over top. Spread some of the mayonnaise on the bun tops and cover. Repeat with the remaining ingredients. Don't forget to wrap the burgers in wax paper (page 123). Let rest for 2 to 3 minutes and serve with Sunny's Hand-Cut Fries and Old Bay Mayonnaise.

ROASTED CHICKEN WITH ROSEMARY AND HONEY MUSTARD GLAZE (SERVES 6)

Every chef knows that a roasted chicken is the most priceless, practical, and perfect thing to have in the fridge. This recipe proves that point. With the right herbs and seasonings, this sandwich will save you on those there's-nothin'-in-the-fridge freak-out moments.

ROSEMARY AND HONEY MUSTARD GLAZE (Makes 1¼ cup)
- 1 cup honey
- ¼ cup Dijon mustard
- 1 tablespoon white wine vinegar
- 1 teaspoon sea salt
- 1 teaspoon freshly ground black pepper

1½ teaspoons chopped fresh rosemary

CHICKEN SANDWICH
- 1 cup plus 1 tablespoon extra virgin olive oil
- 3 cloves garlic, chopped
- ⅓ cup chopped fresh rosemary
- 1 teaspoon sea salt

- 1 teaspoon freshly ground black pepper
- 6 5-ounce boneless, skinless chicken breasts
- 6 potato buns, cut in half
- ½ pound fresh baby spinach
- 2 tomatoes, sliced into thirds
- 1 red onion, thinly sliced

To make the glaze, add the honey, mustard, vinegar, salt, and pepper to a food processor or blender. Puree until smooth. Transfer to a bowl. Stir in the rosemary and mix with a spatula two or three times to incorporate.

To make the sandwich, in a large bowl, combine 1 cup of the oil, the garlic, rosemary, salt, and pepper. Add the chicken, toss to coat, cover, and refrigerate for 1 hour.

Heat the remaining 1 tablespoon of oil in a large skillet over medium heat until the oil starts to sizzle. Remove the chicken from the marinade and pat dry. Increase the heat to medium-high and add the breasts. Cook, turning once, until the chicken is browned, about 20 minutes total. Remove with tongs and place on a platter. Brush the chicken with the glaze.

Toast the buns according to directions on page 123. Set aside.

To assemble the sandwiches, place 1 breast on a bun bottom. Top with some spinach, 1 tomato slice, and some red onion slices. Spread more glaze on the bun top and cover. Repeat with the remaining ingredients. Don't forget to wrap the sandwiches in wax paper (page 123). Let rest for 2 to 3 minutes and serve.

MICHELLE'S
MELT (SERVES 6)

I guess my family knew it wasn't going to be a normal Friday afternoon when they walked up to open the restaurant and found two Secret Service people standing out front. The rest—security checks, the mob scene of customers, flashing cameras, the most gracious First Lady—is a blur now. All they remember is the excitement of meeting Michelle Obama, how sweet her staff was, and how honored we were to even be considered as a stop for her lunch break! All these ingredients can be found in the First Lady's organic garden on the South Lawn of The White House.

TURKEY MIX
2 tablespoons butter
1 cup diced celery
1 cup diced scallions
2 green apples, cored and diced
½ cup canned chipotle chiles in adobo sauce
1 cup store-bought mango chutney

2 pounds ground turkey
¼ cup grated lemon zest
1 teaspoon sea salt
1 teaspoon freshly ground black pepper

CARAMELIZED ONIONS
3 tablespoons canola oil
2 cups thinly sliced Spanish onions

6 slices Swiss cheese
6 leaves iceberg lettuce
6 ruby red tomato slices
Multigrain potato buns, cut in half

Melt the butter in a skillet over medium heat. Add the celery, scallions, and apples. Cook, stirring occasionally, for 15 to 20 minutes. Remove from the heat and set aside. Add the chipotle and ½ tablespoon of adobo sauce from the can and the chutney to a blender. Puree until smooth. Transfer to a bowl.

Add the celery mixture and stir until well combined.

Add the turkey, lemon zest, salt, and pepper and stir until well combined.

To make the patties, roll six 5-ounce turkey balls and form each ball into a patty. Arrange on a tray, cover, and refrigerate.

To make caramelized onions, heat the oil in a large nonstick skillet over medium heat. Add the onions—don't worry if they're piled high; they will cook down. Turn with a spatula so all the onions are evenly coated in oil. Continue to cook, stirring the onions every 8 minutes, until the slices have turned a dark, rich brown color, about 25 minutes. If the onions begin to burn, reduce the heat to medium-low and add more oil. Remove the onions and place them in a bowl.

Heat a large skillet over medium-high heat and add enough just oil to cover the entire bottom. After 2 minutes, reduce the heat to medium and place the patties into the skillet. Season with salt and pepper and cook for 3 minutes. Flip, and cook on the other side for 1 minute.

Place 1 slice cheese on each patty and continue cooking 2 minutes. Cover with a lid for the last 30 seconds to melt the cheese.

Toast the buns according to directions on page 123. Set aside.

To assemble the burgers, place 1 patty on a toasted bun bottom. Top the patty with a tablespoon of caramelized onions, 1 lettuce leaf, 1 tomato slice, and a heaping spoonful of the South Lawn Herb Garden Mayo. Cover with the bun top.

Repeat with the remaining ingredients.

Don't forget to wrap the sandwiches in wax paper (page 123). Let rest for 2 to 3 minutes and serve.

SOUTH LAWN HERB GARDEN MAYO
(MAKES ABOUT 2 CUPS)

- 2 cups mayo (See Homemade Basic Mayonnaise, page 34)
- 2 bunches parsley
- 2 bunches cilantro
- 1 bunch dill
- ½ cup fresh Rosemary
- ½ cup fresh Thyme
- Juice of 8 lemons
- 1 tablespoon minced garlic
- 4 oz salt & pepper mix or to taste
- ¼ cup olive oil

Add all ingredients except for oil to a food processor or blender. Process for 30 seconds in the food processor or 10 seconds in the blender. With the motor running, add the oil in a thin, steady stream until all the oil is added and the mixture is smooth. Stop the motor and taste. If the sauce is too thick, thin it with a little hot water. If too thin, process a little longer. Add lemon, thyme, salt, and pepper. The mayonnaise can be refrigerated in an airtight container for up to 1 week.

STACKED WITH THE
GOOD STUFF (SERVES 6)

I mean, I have to give a shout-out to my fellow Canadian, Mike Green—the ice hockey defense-man for the Washington Capitols of the National Hockey League. Now we're really talking—my two favorite things, ice hockey and burgers! Not only do I love going to the games and watching Mike do his thing, but he was kind enough to create a burger, and let me tell you, he's got some skills in the kitchen too!

30 ounces ground sirloin
 6 potato buns, cut in half
   Canola oil
 6 portobello mushrooms
 2 teaspoons sea salt
 2 teaspoons freshly ground
   black pepper

 6 slices cheddar cheese
 1 cup Chunky Avocado
   Topping (page 135)
 6 leaves iceberg lettuce
12 pickle slices
   About 1 cup Good Stuff
   Sauce (page 35)

To make the patties, roll six 5-ounce sirloin balls and form each ball into a patty. Arrange on a tray, cover, and refrigerate.

Toast the buns according to directions on page 123. Set aside.

Heat a large skillet over medium heat with just enough canola oil to cover the bottom and add the portobello mushrooms. Line a plate with paper towels. Cook, turning once or twice, until fork tender, 3 to 4 minutes. Remove with a slotted spoon. Drain on the paper towels.

Heat the same skillet over medium heat with just enough oil to cover the entire bottom. Place the patties into the skillet. Season the patties with the salt and pepper and cook for 3 minutes. Flip, and cook on the other side for 1 minute. Place 1 slice cheese on each patty and continue to cook 2 minutes more for medium-rare doneness. Cover with a lid for the 30 seconds to melt the cheese.

To assemble the burgers, place 1 patty on 1 toasted bun bottom. Top with 1 heaping tablespoonful of guacamole, 1 lettuce leaf, 1 mushroom, and 2 pickle slices. Dress with some of the sauce. Cover with the bun top. Repeat with the remaining ingredients. Don't forget to wrap the sandwiches in wax paper (page 123). Let rest for 2 to 3 minutes and serve.

© Getty Images

"GOODNESS GRACIOUS, WE HOPE YOU'RE HUNGRY"

REDSKINS #74
SPICY CAJUN BURGER (SERVES 6)

Football players are serious about their food . . . lots and lots of food. So when the Washington Redskins' Justin Geisinger, Stephon Heyer, Casey Rabach, and Chad Rinehart dropped in to Good Stuff Eatery for a special offensive lineman's Quick-Fire challenge, I just knew they'd cook up a storm. What I didn't know is that I'd be arm wrestling Stephon for the recipe!

Heyer, the Redskins' #74 offensive tackle, scored a huge culinary touchdown with his spicy, smoky, juicy burger, loaded with Jack cheese (one of my favorites). Fans could get a peek behind the grill at Good Stuff Eatery and watch Heyer whip up his creation on the NFL Players Helmets Off television series. The #74 Spicy Cajun is the biggest, baddest burger a Redskins fan could dream of.

30 ounces ground sirloin
½ cup Cajun spice blend (see Note)
   Sea salt and freshly ground black pepper
6 potato buns, cut in half

   Canola oil
6 slices pepper Jack cheese
6 leaves iceberg lettuce
6 ruby red tomato slices
6 red onion slices

12 pickle slices
   About 1 cup Good Stuff Sauce (page 35)

To make the patties, in a bowl, combine the sirloin with the Cajun spice blend and salt and pepper and mix well. Roll six 5-ounce sirloin balls and form each ball into a patty. Arrange on a tray, cover, and refrigerate.

Toast the buns according to directions on page 123. Set aside.

Heat a large skillet over medium-high heat and add just enough oil to cover the entire bottom. When the oil begins to smoke, reduce the heat to medium and place the patties into the skillet. Cook the patties for 3 minutes. Flip, and cook on the other side for 1 minute. Place 1 slice cheese on each patty and continue to cook 2 minutes more for medium-rare doneness. Cover with a lid for the last 30 seconds to melt the cheese.

To assemble the burgers, place 1 patty on 1 toasted bun bottom. Top the patty with 1 lettuce leaf, 1 tomato slice, 1 onion slice, and 2 pickle slices. Top with some of the sauce. Cover with the bun top. Repeat with the remaining ingredients. Don't forget to wrap the sandwiches in wax paper (page 123). Let rest for 2 to 3 minutes and serve.

NOTE
You can make your own Cajun spice blend by combining ¼ cup salt, 2 tablespoons cayenne, 2 tablespoons chili powder, 1 tablespoon paprika, 1 tablespoon cracked black pepper, 1 tablespoon garlic powder, and ½ teaspoon ground mustard.

"THE #74 SPICY CAJUN IS THE BIGGEST, BADDEST BURGER A REDSKINS FAN COULD DREAM OF."

HORTON'S KIDS
GRILLED CHEESE (SERVES 4)

I was lucky enough to stumble upon this amazing organization, Horton's Kids, when I first moved to D.C. Created by Karin Walser, the program serves about 165 children in pre-K through grade 12 from the Anacostia section of Washington, D.C.'s Ward 8. Horton's Kids' mission is to "educate and empower the children of Ward 8 by providing comprehensive, direct services which improve the quality of their daily lives and nurture each child's desire and ability to succeed."

Horton's Kids is supported by more than 700 volunteers who tutor the children and take them on weekly field trips. These kids are just fantastic. Good Stuff Eatery has done some great events with them, and their smiles will melt your heart! They've become part of the team. So try out this grilled cheese sandwich, but don't forget to donate first!

Butter, softened
8 **slices potato bread**
16 **slices American cheese**
8 **thin kosher dill pickle slices**

Butter one side of the bread and place buttered side down on a baking sheet or tray. Layer 2 slices of cheese on 4 slices of the bread. Layer 2 kosher dill pickle slices over the cheese. Layer 2 more slices of cheese over the pickles. Top with the remaining bread, buttered side up.

Heat a large nonstick skillet over medium heat. Place 2 sandwiches in the pan and press lightly with a spatula. Toast for 1½ minutes until golden brown on the bottom. Flip, and toast 1 to 2 minutes more, until cheese has melted. Wrap the sandwiches in waxed paper and serve.

© Photography by Scott Henrichsen

BRING ON THE BRAIN FREEZE: SHAKES, MALTS, & FLOAT'S

BIG VERN'S ROOT BEER FLOAT
TOASTED MARSHMALLOW SHAKE
BLACK AND WHITE SHAKE
MILKY WAY MALT
VERY BERRY SHAKE
SOURSOP HOP STRAWBERRY SHAKE
DE-LECHEBLE LECHE
VANILLA AND CHOCOLATE SHAKES
MINT OREO SHAKE
PUMPKIN PATCH SHAKE
CREAMSICLE SHAKE
AVOCADO SHAKE
BANANAS FOSTER SHAKE
PEANUT BUTTER AND JELLY SHAKE
FOR PETE'S SHAKE
CADBURY SHAKE

5

Milkshakes make life better. They bring back childhood **indulgences** with flavors like peanut butter 'n' jelly and of course the score of the century: toasted marshmallow. But you don't need to be a show-off like me: Done right, a simple shake is pure **bliss** through a straw. It's really a no-brainer—bring on brain freeze!

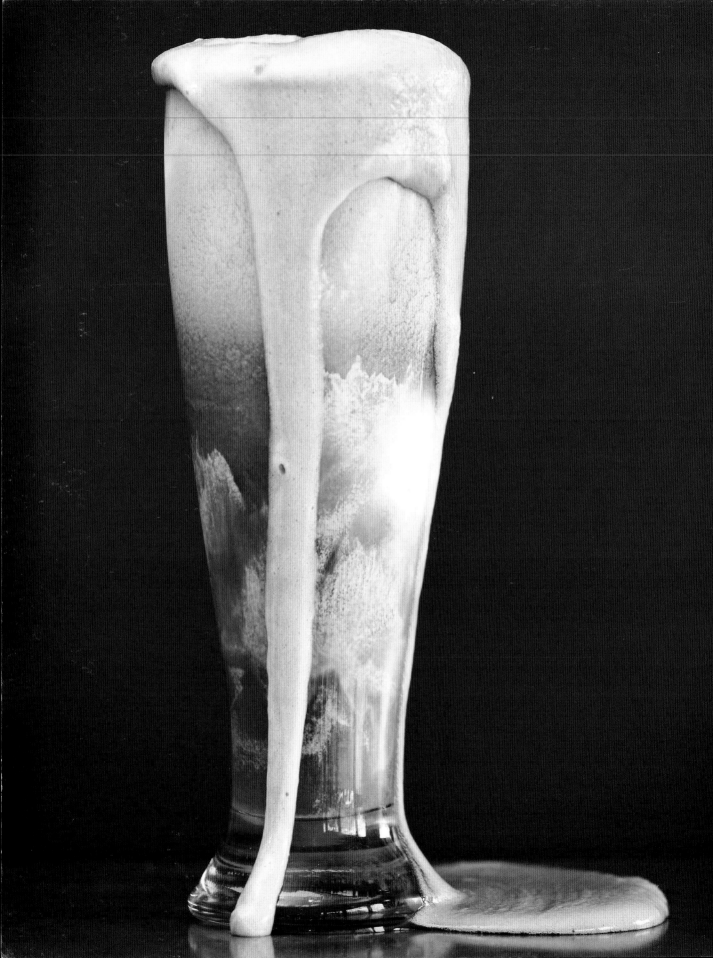

BIG VERN'S
ROOT BEER FLOAT (SERVES 2)

As a special treat after baseball games on Sunday, our contractor Vince McCoullough's father, known as Big Vern, would make "black cows." That is what they were called in the Midwest. It is similar to a root beer float but more ice cream and not quite the consistency of a milk shake. It became a family favorite for them, and soon enough everyone in his neighborhood was drinking this version of a root beer float!

  We had to include his favorite drink. Of course you can make this with just about any soda flavor you'd like.

  2 **scoops creamy vanilla ice cream**
  2 **12-ounce cans root beer**

Add a scoop of ice cream to each of two 16-ounce glasses. Slowly pour the soda over the ice cream. Serve with a straw and/or a spoon.

TOASTED MARSHMALLOW SHAKE (SERVES 4)

This shake is undeniably delicious, but I had no idea it would become, in fact, legendary. We thought of the idea because we're huge marshmallow freaks in my family. Not only is the flavor like a campfire in your mouth, but it evokes those same childhood memories of indulgence and misbehavior! We get mad love for this shake.

- 1 16-ounce bag jumbo marshmallows
- 2 cups whole milk
- 2 cups creamy vanilla ice cream
- 1 tablespoon sour cream

Preheat the broiler.

Reserve 4 marshmallows for garnish. Spread out the remaining marshmallows on a baking sheet in a single layer. Place the sheet under the broiler and cook, stirring once or twice, until completely charred, 2 to 3 minutes. Remove from the oven and set aside to cool.

Repeat with the remaining 4 marshmallows, but cook just until toasted slightly golden, about 1 minute. Remove from the oven and set aside to cool.

Add the milk, ice cream, sour cream, and burnt marshmallows to a blender. Blend for 5 minutes. Pour into four 8-ounce glasses and garnish each glass with a golden marshmallow.

WHIPPED CREAM (MAKES ENOUGH FOR 4 MILKSHAKES)

Light, fluffy, simply delicious.

1 cup chilled heavy cream
¼ cup confectioners' sugar
1 teaspoon vanilla extract

Whip the cream using an upright mixer with a balloon whisk or a handheld electric beater until almost stiff. Gradually add the sugar, beating until well mixed. Add the vanilla. Beat until the cream holds peaks. Top shakes with dollops of the whipped cream.

BLACK AND WHITE SHAKE (SERVES 4)

My mother's favorite shake. Enough said.

1 cup hot fudge sauce
2 cups creamy vanilla ice cream
1 cup whole milk
Whipped Cream
(page 178)

Reserve 4 teaspoons of the hot fudge sauce and divide and drizzle the remaining sauce down the sides of each of four 8-ounce glasses. Twirl the glasses around to coat the insides. Add the ice cream and milk to a blender and blend until smooth, about 30 seconds. Pour into the prepared glasses. Garnish each with a dollop of whipped cream and 1 teaspoon hot fudge sauce.

THE CUSTARD

My mother's grandfather, Nicholas Sklavounakis or "Nick Nakis," came to Canada in 1917, at 14 years old. He was a stowaway on a Vergotis ship headed for Cuba to pick up a load of sugarcane and transport it to Canada. While on the ship, he worked in the kitchen with a friend. His friend fell asleep in the coal rooms and when the ship docked in Cuba my great-grandfather couldn't find him. So he got nervous and stayed on the ship; next stop—Canada. As the ship came up the St. Lawrence River, both jumped off and swam to shore. His first job was at the Windsor train station as a night watchman for a restaurant. In addition to cleaning and guarding, he also spun thick ice cream, which he loved to eat a little of every night.

At Good Stuff Eatery we make our own custard base, every morning. That's what gives our shakes an amazing consistency and makes people keep coming back for more.

MILKY WAY
MALT (SERVES 4)

We grew up in Montreal, so hockey's what we lived for. Forget baseball and football, we woke up at 5 A.M., put on a thousand pounds of uniform, and hit the rink. I was the goalie in our peewee club. The only problem was my way to stop the puck was to just fall on it; I figured this was the best approach. Well, it turned out to be a kinda smart move because most kids couldn't hit the puck too high, but when I left I was seriously bruised up. The recovery: a Milky Way bar after each game.

¼ cup hot fudge sauce
¼ cup butterscotch sauce
1½ cups malt balls
 2 cups creamy vanilla ice
    cream
    Whipped Cream
    (page 178)

In a small bowl, combine 1 tablespoon of the hot fudge sauce with 1 tablespoon of the butterscotch sauce and drizzle them down the sides of an 8-ounce glass. Twirl the glass around to coat the inside. Repeat with three more glasses.

Add the malt balls to a blender and pulse until they are crushed but not powdery. Alternatively, place them in a plastic bag and pound with a mallet just enough to crush them. Set aside 4 teaspoons for garnish.

Add the ice cream to the crushed malt balls in the blender and blend until smooth, about 30 seconds. Pour into the prepared glasses. Garnish each with a dollop of whipped cream and 1 teaspoon of the reserved crushed malt balls.

VERY BERRY
SHAKE (SERVES 4)

In theory, my handsome, fit, young-for-his-age father tries to eat healthily. He doesn't think twice about anything made by my mother (who would!), but outside her kitchen, he's pretty cautious. That said, we created a shake that kinda, sorta sounds and is nutritious, so that health nuts everywhere could gobble it up, guilt-free. Perception is reality, right?!

2 cups seasonal berries,
   one variety or a mix
2 cups creamy vanilla ice
   cream
1 cup whole milk

Set aside 8 berries for garnish. Add the remaining berries, ice cream, and milk to a blender and puree until smooth. Pour into four 8-ounce glasses and garnish each with 2 berries.

SOURSOP HOP STRAWBERRY SHAKE (SERVES 4)

Soursop is a fruit I first tried while traveling in the Caribbean. I love the clash of sour and sweet, but more than anything, I love how this name rolls up your tongue. Try saying it ten times in a row . . .

A popular tropical fruit native to Mexico, the Caribbean, and Central America, soursop tastes a little like creamy strawberries with a hint of pineapple and maybe coconut. It's also commonly known as guanábana. Look for soursop puree in Hispanic markets.

- **2 cups hulled and sliced strawberries**
- **2 cups creamy vanilla ice cream**
- **½ cup soursop puree**
- **2 tablespoons sour cream**
  Whipped Cream
  (page 178)

Combine the strawberries, ice cream, soursop, and sour cream in a blender and puree until smooth. Pour the mixture into four 8-ounce glasses and garnish each with a dollop of whipped cream.

"WHO SAYS YOU CAN'T WAKE UP TO A SHAKE?"

DE-LECHEBLE
LECHE (SERVES 4)

My mom has a first-cousins club. It includes Chris-Ann, Tassie, and Suzy; they all grew up together in Montreal. They meet up all the time and developed their own little Red Hat Society, which includes them dressing up in bright red hats and purple shawls. During one of these meet ups, my mom mentioned how she wanted to open another kitchen shop—Mom's first business, at 25 years old, was a kitchen shop in Montreal's famed Queen Elizabeth Hotel. Anyway, Suzy volunteered to visit Mom for a weekend to brainstorm a kitchen shop, which then turned into a sandwich shop, and by Sunday was a hamburger joint. Since I was in New York and my sister was busy with her job, Suzy committed to helping out for a couple of months, to jump-start the business, and ended up staying for 10 months—I'm not joking. Not only did she come up with this shake, she also helped conceive the name and the concept of the restaurant with my parents. Look for dulce de leche syrup at supermarkets and specialty food stores.

1 cup butterscotch sauce
2 cups creamy vanilla ice
   cream
1 cup whole milk
½ cup dulce de leche syrup

Whipped Cream
   (page 178)
4 tablespoons ground
   coffee

Drizzle 2 tablespoons of the butterscotch sauce down the sides of each of four 8-ounce glasses. Twirl the glasses around to coat the insides.

Add the remaining butterscotch sauce, ice cream, milk, and dulce de leche syrup to a blender and blend until smooth, about 30 seconds. Pour into the prepared glasses. Garnish each with a dollop of whipped cream and sprinkle 1 tablespoon ground coffee over the top.

VANILLA AND CHOCOLATE SHAKES (EACH SERVES 4)

There is nothing more therapeutic than an old-fashioned vanilla or chocolate shake. Just recently, I felt utterly overwhelmed with life. Instead of my usual Spike-self-help methods like writing to-do lists or taking a walk, I simply ordered a chocolate shake, sat on a park bench, and sipped in silence; suddenly, life seemed better.

VANILLA SHAKE

- 2 cups creamy vanilla ice cream
- 1 cup whole milk
  Whipped cream (page 178)
- 4 maraschino cherries, for garnish

Add the ice cream and milk to a blender and blend until smooth, about 30 seconds. Pour into four 8-ounce glasses. Garnish each with a dollop of whipped cream and a cherry.

CHOCOLATE SHAKE

- 2 cups creamy chocolate ice cream
- 1 cup whole milk
  Whipped cream (page 178)
- 4 maraschino cherries, for garnish

Add the ice cream and milk to a blender and blend until smooth, about 30 seconds. Pour into four 8-ounce glasses. Garnish each with a dollop of whipped cream and a cherry.

MINT OREO
SHAKE (SERVES 4)

When I was a teenager, I tended to skip class now and then. Shocker! One of my favorite places to go while playing hooky was Friendly's, where I'd get either a mint chocolate chip cone or a cookies 'n' cream one. This recipe would have been my teenage fantasy—complete with a surfboard and a beautiful model by my side!

20 **Oreo mint creme cookies**
 2 **cups creamy vanilla ice
    cream**
 1 **cup whole milk
    Whipped cream
    (page 178)**

Reserve 4 cookies for garnish. Add the remaining cookies to a food processor or blender and process to a powder, about 1 minute. Add the ice cream and milk and blend until smooth, about 30 seconds. Pour into four 8-ounce glasses. Garnish each with a dollop of whipped cream and a cookie.

PUMPKIN PATCH
SHAKE (SERVES 4)

I love seasonal cooking, so whenever a season changes and a holiday week comes up, I try to think of a culinary way to honor the holiday. We thought about putting this killer on our permanent menu, but we decided that some things are better left sacred, for special occasions only.

1 15-ounce can pumpkin puree
2 cups creamy vanilla ice cream
1 cup whole milk
1 cup graham cracker crumbs
2 tablespoons pumpkin pie spice
Whipped cream (page 178)

Add the pumpkin puree, ice cream, milk, graham cracker crumbs, and pumpkin pie spice to a blender and blend until smooth and silky, about 30 seconds. Pour into four 8-ounce glasses. Garnish each with a dollop of whipped cream.

SPICE UP YOUR AFTERNOON CHEERS!

CREAMSICLE
SHAKE (SERVES 4)

When I was living in Brooklyn, broke but happy, I'd buy Creamsicles from the corner bodega to brighten my overworked, underpaid existence. This tradition really started with my mother, whose favorite dessert was a Creamsicle. So, I grew up eating them for dessert: you know, quintessential feel-good food. This shake is a guaranteed smile, whether you're slummin' it in Brooklyn or sunbathing in Beverly Hills.

1 orange
1 cup orange cream soda
½ cup orange sherbet
1 cup creamy vanilla ice
   cream
½ cup whole milk
   Whipped cream
   (page 178)

Using a sharp paring knife, cut the rind off the orange, starting at one end and following the contours of the orange, so you have 4 pieces of orange rind. Set aside.

   Add the peeled orange, cream soda, sherbet, ice cream, and milk in a blender and blend until smooth, about 30 seconds. Pour into four 8-ounce glasses. Garnish each with a dollop of whipped cream and 1 orange rind piece.

AVOCADO
SHAKE (SERVES 4)

I know what you're thinking: no thank you! Let me explain why you should attempt this recipe. One of my buddies made an avocado shaved ice once, and it was outstanding. This takes it to a new level.

4 ripe avocados
1 14-ounce can sweetened
   condensed milk
2 cups creamy vanilla ice
   cream

½ cup whole milk
   Whipped cream
   (page 178)

Cut each avocado in half, discard the pits, and scoop out the meat. Add to a blender and blend until finely chopped, about 1 minute. Add the remaining ingredients, reserving 6 teaspoons chopped cilantro for garnish. Blend until smooth, about 30 seconds.

Pour into four 8-ounce glasses. Garnish each with a dollop of whipped cream.

BANANAS FOSTER
SHAKE (SERVES 4)

No-brainer. You can omit the rum, but it adds a pleasant kick and it tastes delicious.

- 1 tablespoon butter
- 4 bananas, sliced into ½-inch-thick circles
- 1 cup dark brown sugar
- ½ cup dark rum
- 2 cups crushed vanilla wafers

- 2 cups creamy vanilla ice cream
- 1 cup whole milk
- Whipped cream (page 178)

Heat the butter in a skillet over high heat. Add the bananas and brown sugar and cook, turning occasionally, just until the edges of the bananas begin to burn, about 4 minutes. Add the rum and stir. Transfer to a blender, add the wafers, ice cream, and milk, and blend until smooth, about 30 seconds. Pour into four 8-ounce glasses. Garnish each with a dollop of whipped cream.

PEANUT BUTTER AND JELLY
SHAKE (SERVES 4)

Comfort food is my favorite food genre. If I'm overtired or just a little off my game, peanut butter and jelly cradles me right back to myself. Combine that with a shake, and I'm as happy as a pig in (sticky grape) mud.

- 2 cups creamy vanilla ice cream
- 2 cups creamy peanut butter
- 1½ cups Concord grape jelly

- 1 cup whole milk
- ½ cup crushed peanut butter cookies
- Whipped cream (page 178)

Add the ice cream, peanut butter, jelly, milk, and crushed cookies to a blender and blend until smooth, about 30 seconds. Pour into four 8-ounce glasses. Garnish each with a dollop of whipped cream.

"FOR THE ROMANTIC IN US ALL"

FOR PETE'S
SHAKE (SERVES 4)

Here's to the Don of the Polatos family, who always believed in Good Stuff!

3 ounces semisweet
  chocolate, chopped
12 large, fresh cherries with
  stems
2 cups creamy chocolate
  ice cream

½ cup whole milk
½ cup maraschino cherries
  Whipped cream
  (page 178)

Line a baking sheet with wax paper. Place the chocolate in the top of a double boiler set over barely simmering water (do not allow the bottom of the pan to touch the water). Stir until melted and smooth. Remove the top of the double boiler from over the water. Holding a cherry stem, dip a cherry halfway into the chocolate. Place the cherry, chocolate side down, on the prepared sheet. Repeat with the remaining cherries and chocolate. Refrigerate until the chocolate is firm, at least 15 minutes. (If you don't want to use a double boiler, put the chocolate in a bowl with 2 teaspoons of milk and melt in the microwave, about 2 minutes. Stir until completely melted. Save leftover chocolate for another use.)

Add the ice cream, milk, and maraschino cherries to a blender and blend until smooth, about 30 seconds. Pour into four 8-ounce glass. Garnish each with a dollop of whipped cream and the chocolate cherries.

CADBURY
SHAKE (SERVES 4)

This shake is a fun twist for the child in all of us.

2 Cadbury Creme Eggs
½ cup butterscotch sauce
½ cup chocolate sauce

6 cups creamy chocolate
   ice cream
Whipped cream
   (page 178)

Cut each chocolate egg in half lengthwise and set aside.

Drizzle 1 tablespoon of the butterscotch sauce down the sides of each of four 8-ounce glasses. Twirl the glasses around to coat on the inside. Repeat with the chocolate sauce.

Add the remaining butterscotch sauce and ice cream to a blender and blend until smooth, about 30 seconds. Pour into the prepared glasses. Garnish each with a dollop of whipped cream and an egg half.

DON'T BELIEVE WHAT THEY SAY, I'M A SWEETHEART: DESSERTS

GREEK YOGURT WITH HONEY AND NUTS
OATMEAL AND MILK CHOCOLATE COOKIES
RED VELVET BROWNIES WITH WHITE CHOCOLATE ICING
COCONUT-MERINGUE DARK CHOCOLATE BROWNIES
CARROT CAKE WITH CREAM CHEESE ICING
CINNAMON-CHOCOLATE BROWNIES
BANANA-CHOCOLATE COOKIE SANDWICHES
CHEESECAKE-BLUEBERRY BLONDIES
CHERRY-APRICOT JAM BLONDIES
RASPBERRY SUGAR COOKIES
BAKLAVA COOKIES
HONEY—PINE NUT BARS
VIETNAMESE COFFEE BROWNIES
GOOD STUFF POPSICLES
CALVADOS CANDY APPLES
CARDAMOM AND CARAMEL POPCORN
LOUKOU BEIGNETS
POMEGRANATE GRANITA
CARLA'S PUMPKIN TRIFLE
BIRTHDAY CAKE

6

Sweet toothers unite! This chapter embraces the sugar-rush chasers, choc-oholics, pie-fighting maniacs, raw **cookie** dough–munchers, **buttercream** freaks, cheesecake-for-breakfast nuts, midnight brownie bakers, and closet carrot **cake**–loving addicts. Lick your beaters and get naughty.

"GREEKS MAKE YOGURT—
WE DON'T BUY IT. IT'S
AGAINST OUR RELIGION."

GREEK YOGURT WITH HONEY AND NUTS (SERVES 4)

When my sister, Micheline, visits our home on the gorgeous island, Kefalonia, in Greece, every day she walks down to our village café, Marina's, and orders this delicious treat. It's her favorite and I don't think I could have ever written a cookbook without including it.

GREEK YOGURT
- 12 cups whole milk
- 1 cup plain yogurt

TOPPINGS
- 4 tablespoons honey
- 4 teaspoons chopped mixed nuts, such as almonds and walnuts, or trail mix

To make the yogurt, heat the milk in a saucepan over medium heat for 45 minutes. Pour into a plastic bowl. Let cool to lukewarm, or until a skin forms on the surface. Discard the skin.

Mix in the yogurt. Cover the pan and place in a warm, dry place until it thickens, 8 to 12 hours or overnight. Place in a cheesecloth square or even (my grandmother does this) a pillow case, and drain over a bowl. Allow to drain for 2 hours. Refrigerate for 4 hours before using.

To serve, spoon desired portions of the yogurt into four bowls; refrigerate any unused portion. Pour the honey over the yogurt and sprinkle with the nuts. Serve immediately.

OATMEAL AND MILK CHOCOLATE COOKIES (MAKES 24 COOKIES)

I know a New York City girl who buys all her meals out and uses the stove as storage for Hermès scarves, which is why I almost passed out when she brought these scrumptious cookies to work one day. The recipe is easy and unintimidating, which is what tempted her to try it in the first place.

1¼ cups all-purpose flour
½ teaspoon baking powder
½ teaspoon baking soda
¼ teaspoon salt
¾ cup (1½ sticks) unsalted butter, softened

¾ cup packed dark brown sugar
1 large egg
1½ teaspoons vanilla extract
1½ cups milk chocolate chips

1 cup rolled oats
2 tablespoons half-and-half

Preheat the oven to 350°F.

In a mixing bowl, sift together the flour, baking powder, baking soda, and salt. In another bowl, beat together the butter, brown sugar, egg, and vanilla with an electric mixer until creamy. Stir in the chocolate chips and oats. Fold in the flour mixture and the half-and-half. Drop the dough by the tablespoonful onto ungreased baking sheets.

Bake for 10 minutes, or until the edges are crisp. Cool on the baking sheets for a few minutes and enjoy.

RED VELVET BROWNIES WITH WHITE CHOCOLATE ICING
(MAKES 12 BROWNIES)

These will make anything alright. Always.

RED VELVET BROWNIES
2½ cups cake flour, plus more for the pan
2 tablespoons unsweetened cocoa powder
1 teaspoon baking powder
½ teaspoon salt
1 cup semisweet chocolate chips

3 large eggs
14 tablespoons (1 3/4 sticks) unsalted butter, plus more for the pan, softened
1 cup confectioners' sugar
1 cup buttermilk
2 tablespoons red food coloring
1 teaspoon white vinegar
1 teaspoon baking soda

1 teaspoon vanilla extract
WHITE CHOCOLATE FROSTING
1 cup sweetened condensed milk
8 tablespoons (1 stick) unsalted butter
8 ounces (about 1⅓ cups) white chocolate chips
3 large egg yolks, beaten
1 cup confectioners' sugar

Preheat the oven to 325°F. Butter and flour a 9-inch square baking pan.

To make the brownies, combine the flour, cocoa, baking powder, and salt in the top of a double boiler over boiling water (do not allow the bottom of the pan to touch the water). Add the chocolate chips and cook, stirring, until the chocolate melts and the mixture is smooth. Remove and let cool for 10 minutes.

In a large bowl, combine the eggs, butter, and ½ cup water. Add the confectioners' sugar, buttermilk, food coloring, vinegar, baking soda, and vanilla. Beat the mixture with an electric mixer until smooth. Stir in the chocolate mixture. Pour the mixture into the prepared pan.

Bake for 40 minutes, or until the top is set and a knife inserted in the center comes out clean. Remove from the oven and set the pan on a rack to cool.

Meanwhile, to make the frosting, heat the condensed milk, butter, and chocolate chips in a saucepan over medium heat. Cook, stirring constantly, until the chocolate chips melt. Remove from the heat and let cool. In a mixing bowl, beat together the egg yolks and confectioners' sugar with an electric mixer until fluffy. Add the chocolate mixture and beat until thick. When the brownies are cool, spread the frosting over top.

COCONUT-MERINGUE DARK CHOCOLATE BROWNIES
(MAKES 12 BROWNIES)

I'm not going to lie. I was having way too much fun in Jamaica once and might have had some insatiable food cravings. I fortuitously found these brownies at a street stand and made a mental note to self to replicate them when I got home. Somehow I remembered my mission and we whipped up this identical recipe. Don't worry, be happy!

BROWNIES

- 4 ounces unsweetened dark chocolate, coarsely chopped
- 6 tablespoons (¾ stick) unsalted butter, plus more for the pan
- ⅔ cup all-purpose flour, plus more for the pan
- ½ teaspoon baking powder
- ¼ teaspoon salt
- 1 cup sugar
- 2 large eggs
- 1 teaspoon vanilla extract

COCONUT MERINGUE

- 4 large egg whites
- ½ cup sugar
- ½ teaspoon vanilla extract
- ½ teaspoon coconut extract or 2 tablespoons shredded coconut

Preheat the oven to 350°F. Butter and flour an 8-inch square baking pan.

To make the brownies, heat the chocolate and butter in a saucepan over medium heat. Cook, stirring constantly, until melted and smooth; do not overheat. Remove from heat and cool to room temperature.

In a small bowl, combine the flour, baking powder, and salt. In another bowl, beat together the sugar, eggs, and vanilla with an electric mixer until the mixture is very thick. Whisk the melted chocolate mixture into the sugar-egg mixture, then stir in the flour mixture. Pour into the prepared pan. Bake the brownies for about 20 minutes, or until the top is set and a knife inserted in the center comes out clean.

Meanwhile, to make the meringue, in a clean, dry bowl, beat the egg whites with an electric mixer until fluffy. Gradually add the sugar, vanilla, and coconut extract, and beat until stiff and glossy. When the brownies are done, pour the meringue over top. Increase the heat to broil and brown the meringue topping. Remove from the oven and cool before slicing.

CARROT CAKE WITH CREAM CHEESE ICING (SERVES 8)

The Hamptons is not my ideal scene. It's a little too uptight for untucked me. However, a friend once invited me to a dinner party where the dessert outshined even the most expensive jewels and sports cars. This plate of heaven brought everyone back down to earth!

CARROT CAKE
Butter for the pan
4 large eggs
2 cups confectioners' sugar
2 cups cake flour, plus more for the pan
1½ cups canola oil
2 teaspoons baking soda
3 cups finely shredded carrots
½ cup sweetened flaked coconut
1 teaspoon vanilla extract
Pinch salt

CREAM CHEESE ICING
6 ounces (12 tablespoons) cream cheese, at room temperature
1 tablespoon unsalted butter, softened
1¼ cups confectioners' sugar
½ teaspoon vanilla extract

Preheat the oven to 350°F. Butter and flour a 9-inch square baking pan.

To make the carrot cake, in a bowl, beat together the eggs, confectioners' sugar, flour, canola oil, and baking soda with an electric mixer to mix. Stir in the carrots, coconut, vanilla, and salt and mix well. Spoon the batter into the prepared pan.

Bake for 30 minutes, or until a knife inserted in the center comes out clean. Remove from the oven and set the pan on a rack to cool.

Meanwhile, to make the icing, in a large bowl, beat together the cream cheese and butter with an electric mixer until creamy. Gradually add the confectioners' sugar and vanilla, and beat until smooth. When the cake is cool, spread the icing over top.

CINNAMON-CHOCOLATE
BROWNIES (MAKES 24 BROWNIES)

Log cabins, hot cocoa, and ski bunnies, anyone? If I close my eyes I can just taste our trips to the Laurentian Mountains . . .

½ cup all-purpose flour
1½ teaspoons ground cinnamon, plus more for sprinkling
½ teaspoon cayenne
⅛ teaspoon salt
8 ounces semisweet chocolate chips

¾ cup (1½ sticks) unsalted butter, plus more for the pan, softened
4 large eggs
1 cup confectioners' sugar
1½ teaspoons vanilla extract
Whipped Cream (page 178)

Preheat the oven to 350°F. Butter and flour a 9-inch square baking pan.

To make the brownies, into a small bowl, sift together the flour, cinnamon, cayenne, and salt. Heat the chocolate chips and butter in a saucepan over medium heat. Cook, stirring until melted and smooth. Remove from the heat.

In a large bowl, beat together the eggs, sugar, and vanilla with an electric mixer until stiff, about 5 minutes. Gradually add the flour mixture and mix well. Gradually beat in the chocolate mixture until just mixed in. Pour the batter into the prepared pan.

Bake for about 35 minutes, or until the top is set and a knife inserted into the center comes out clean. Remove from the oven and set the pan on a rack to cool completely before slicing.

Meanwhile, make the Whipped Cream. Top the cooled brownies with dollops of fresh whipped cream and add a sprinkle of cinnamon.

BANANA-CHOCOLATE COOKIE SANDWICHES (MAKES 20 COOKIES)

My dad goes bananas for bananas. We have to hide these cookies from him because he'll hoard the entire tray.

COOKIES
- 2 cups sugar
- 1 cup (2 sticks) unsalted butter, softened
- 2 large eggs
- 5 very ripe bananas, mashed
- 2 teaspoons baking soda
- 4 cups all-purpose flour
- 1 teaspoon salt
- 1 teaspoon ground cinnamon
- 1 teaspoon ground cloves

CHOCOLATE FILLING
- 6 ounces (12 tablespoons) cream cheese, at room temperature
- 3 tablespoons half-and-half
- 2 cups sugar
- 2 ounces unsweetened chocolate, melted and cooled

Preheat the oven to 350°F. Line a baking sheet with parchment.

To make the cookies, in a mixing bowl, beat together the sugar and butter with an electric mixer until well mixed. Add the eggs and beat until the mixture is light and fluffy. In another bowl, mix together the bananas and baking soda and let sit for 2 minutes.

In a bowl, sift together the flour, salt, cinnamon, and cloves. Fold into the butter mixture. Stir the flour-butter mixture into the bananas and mix just until combined. Drop by tablespoonfuls onto the prepared baking sheet.

Bake for 15 minutes, or until golden brown. Remove from the oven and set the sheet on a rack to cool.

Meanwhile, to make the filling, in a bowl, beat together the cream cheese and half-and-half with an electric mixer. Add the sugar, 1 cup at a time, blending well after each addition. Stir in the chocolate and beat until smooth.

When the cookies are cool, frost one cookie with the chocolate filling, and press a second cookie on top to form a sandwich. Repeat with the rest of the ingredients.

CHEESECAKE-BLUEBERRY BLONDIES (MAKES 12 BLONDIES)

Cheesecake isn't my thing. (Sorry!) However, these converted me.

1½ cups all-purpose flour, plus more for the pan
½ cup sugar
6 ounces (12 tablespoons) cream cheese, at room temperature

1 teaspoon vanilla extract
1 large egg yolk
6 tablespoons (¾ stick) unsalted butter, plus more for the pan
1 cup white chocolate

chips, optional
⅓ cup blueberry preserves

Preheat the oven to 350°F. Butter and flour a 9-inch square baking pan.

In a bowl, beat together the flour, sugar, cream cheese, and vanilla with an electric mixer until smooth. Beat in the egg yolk until combined. Set aside. Melt the butter and chocolate chips, if using, in a saucepan or in the microwave. Stir into the cream cheese mixture and mix well. Pour into the prepared pan.

Heat the preserves in a saucepan over medium-high heat until it softens and thins. Drizzle the preserves over the batter with a spoon.

Bake for 30 to 35 minutes, or until the top is set and a knife inserted in the center comes out clean. Let cool on a rack before slicing, and enjoy.

CHERRY-APRICOT JAM
BLONDIES (MAKES 12 BLONDIES)

I have a cherry blossom tree, Fred, in front of my D.C. brownstone. I'm madly in love with Fred—just thought I'd tell you that. He's old, beautiful, and was the inspiration for these goodies.

1½ cups all-purpose flour,
    plus more for the pan
½ cup sugar
6 ounces (12 tablespoons)
    cream cheese, at room
    temperature
1 teaspoon vanilla extract

1 large egg yolk
6 tablespoons (¾ stick)
    unsalted butter, plus
    more for the pan
1 cup white chocolate
    chips, optional
⅓ cup cherry preserves

⅓ cup apricot preserves

Preheat the oven to 350°F. Butter and flour a 9-inch square baking pan.

In a bowl, beat together the flour, sugar, cream cheese, and vanilla with an electric mixer until smooth. Beat in the egg yolk to mix. Set aside.

Melt the butter and chocolate chips, if using, in a saucepan or in the microwave. Stir into the cream cheese mixture. Pour into the prepared pan.

Heat the cherry preserves in one saucepan and the apricot preserves in another over medium-high heat until they soften and thin. Drizzle the preserves over the batter with a spoon.

Bake for 30 to 35 minutes, or until the top is golden and a knife inserted in the center comes out clean. Let cool on a rack before slicing, and enjoy.

RASPBERRY SUGAR COOKIES (MAKES 24 COOKIES)

When we'd go raspberry picking as kids, I'd turn into a little devil. Literally and figuratively. I'd come back covered in red, with my entire winnings in my tummy, trying to cover up the fact that I ate my way through the fields. To this day, I get a rush every time I bake these—and I think my parents get nightmares.

2¾ cups all-purpose flour
1 teaspoon baking soda
½ teaspoon baking powder
1½ cups sugar
1 cup (2 sticks)
   unsalted butter,
   softened

1 large egg
1 teaspoon vanilla extract
½ cup seedless raspberry
   preserves

Preheat the oven to 350°F.

In a bowl, sift together the flour, baking soda, and baking powder. In another bowl, beat together the sugar and butter with an electric mixer until smooth. Beat in the egg and vanilla. Slowly blend in the flour mixture.

Using your hands, form small, round dough balls and place them on ungreased baking sheets. Press down with your thumb into each ball to make an indentation. Place 1 teaspoon preserves into the center of each cookie.

Bake for 10 minutes, or until golden. Let stand on the sheets for 2 minutes before removing to cool on wire racks.

BAKLAVA COOKIES (MAKES 24 COOKIES)

Easy one. I'm Greek. This dessert is as essential as the air we breathe!

COOKIES
- 2¾ cups all-purpose flour
- 1½ cups chopped walnuts
- 1 teaspoon ground cinnamon
- 1 teaspoon baking soda
- ½ teaspoon baking powder
- ½ teaspoon salt
- 1¼ cups (2½ sticks) unsalted butter, softened
- 2 cups sugar
- 1 large egg
- 1 teaspoon vanilla extract

GLAZE
- ⅓ cup honey
- 2 tablespoons unsalted butter, softened
- 1 teaspoon vanilla extract
- ½ teaspoon fresh lemon juice
- ¼ teaspoon ground cinnamon

Preheat the oven to 350°F.

To make the cookies, in a bowl, mix together the flour, walnuts, cinnamon, baking soda, baking powder, and salt. In a second bowl, beat together the butter and sugar with an electric mixer until smooth. Beat in the egg and vanilla. Slowly blend in the flour-nut mixture.

Using your hands, form small, round dough balls and place them on ungreased baking sheets. Gently press down on the balls to slightly flatten each cookie.

To make the glaze, heat the honey, butter, vanilla, lemon juice, and cinnamon in a large saucepan over low heat until syrupy. Set aside until ready to use.

Bake the cookies for 10 minutes, or until golden. Remove from the oven and drizzle the glaze over the cookies. Let stand on the sheets until cooled completely.

HONEY–PINE NUT BARS (MAKES 24 BARS)

Every year I make a visit to this wonderful family that lives in Kaminarata, Lixouri (part of the island of Kefalonia); they supply me with honey while I'm in Greece, and of course I bring a jar back to enjoy in the States. My favorite part of the visits is the grandmother who comes shuffling out with a spoonful of the new honey for me to taste. They also have delicious sweets, and here's one of my favorites.

¾ cup (1½ sticks) unsalted butter, softened but cool, plus 3 tablespoons cut into several pieces, plus more for the pan
⅓ cup granulated sugar
½ teaspoon salt
½ cup rolled oats
1¾ cups all-purpose flour
½ cup honey
½ cup packed light brown sugar
⅓ cup heavy cream
2 cups chopped pine nuts
½ teaspoon vanilla extract

Preheat the oven to 350°F. Butter a 9-inch square baking pan.

Cream the 12 tablespoons softened butter, sugar, and salt in a large bowl with a wooden spoon. Stir in the oats. Stir in one-third of the flour at a time, rubbing in the last bit of it by hand to make coarse crumbs. Sprinkle in 1 tablespoon of cold water and rub briefly. Press the dough into the pan. Bake for 15 minutes, or until golden. Remove and let cool.

Meanwhile, combine the honey, brown sugar, cream, and 3 tablespoons butter in a saucepan. Bring the mixture to a boil. Boil for 1 minute. Remove from the heat and stir in the pine nuts and vanilla. Immediately pour over baked crust, spreading evenly with a spoon.

Bake for 15 minutes more. Remove and let cool in the pan on a rack. Cover and refrigerate the bars for 1 to 2 hours before slicing.

VIETNAMESE COFFEE
BROWNIES (MAKES 12 BROWNIES)

Vietnamese coffee is completely addictive! I try to incorporate the flavor into everything I can! Considering I'm a chef, if this is my only vice, we're doing just fine.

- 1 cup sugar
- ½ cup (1 stick) unsalted butter, plus more for the pan, softened
- 2 large eggs
- 1 teaspoon vanilla extract
- ¾ cup milk chocolate pieces, chopped
- ½ cup all-purpose flour, plus more for the pan
- ⅓ cup unsweetened cocoa powder
- ¼ cup canola oil
- ¼ cup coffee liqueur
- ¼ teaspoon salt
- ¼ teaspoon baking powder
- ¼ cup strong ground coffee

Preheat the oven to 350°F. Butter and flour an 8-inch square baking pan.

In a large bowl, beat the sugar, butter, eggs, and vanilla with an electric mixer until smooth. Fold in the chocolate, flour, cocoa, oil, liqueur, salt, and baking powder. Spread the batter into the prepared pan.

Bake for 25 minutes, or until the top is set and a knife inserted into the center comes out clean; do not overbake. Remove from the oven and set the pan on a rack to cool. Sprinkle with ground coffee.

GOOD STUFF POPSICLES (MAKES 6 POPSICLES)

Usually around midnight, I open my freezer and laugh. Why? Because I'm searching for a popsicle. Yes, that's right, me, the chef trained in France, disciplined at Le Cirque and Bouchon, prefers popsicles to petits fours any night of the week. I might have a purple tongue, but I'm not apologizing!

1 cup sugar
⅓ cup chopped fresh
   rosemary
1 tablespoon light corn
   syrup
   Grated zest from 2
   lemons
1 cup fresh lemon juice,
   strained

Heat the sugar with 1 cup water in a saucepan over medium heat. Cook, stirring occasionally, until the sugar has completely dissolved. Add the rosemary, corn syrup, and lemon zest. Increase the heat to medium and bring to a simmer. Remove from the heat and let cool.

Add the lemon juice to a bowl. Add the cooled simple syrup to the lemon juice, straining out the lemon zest as you pour the syrup into the juice. Pour the lemon mixture into popsicle molds. Freeze for at least 4 hours. To unmold, run under hot water for a few seconds.

CALVADOS CANDY
APPLES (MAKES 8 APPLES)

Calvados is an apple brandy made in Normandy. While studying in France, I had a stroke of genius: this combined with candy apples could make me a millionaire. Cha-chingggg! Emeril—what?! Martha—who?!

8 wooden sticks
  Butter for the baking
  sheet
1 kitchen syringe
8 medium apples,
  stems removed

1 cup Calvados
3 cups sugar
½ cup dark corn syrup
¼ teaspoon ground
  cinnamon

Insert a wooden stick into the end of each apple. Generously butter a baking sheet. Using a kitchen syringe, inject each apple with 1 ounce of the Calvados. Set the apples aside.

Heat 1 cup of water, the sugar, and corn syrup in a saucepan over medium heat. Cook, stirring, until the sugar has dissolved. Boil for 15 minutes. Remove from the heat and stir in the cinnamon.

Dip one apple completely in the syrup and swirl it around a little with the stick to coat. Hold the apple up to drain off excess. Place the apple, with the stick facing up, on the prepared baking sheet. Repeat with the remaining apples. Let cool completely before serving.

"POPCORN AND A MOVIE? ACTUALLY, JUST POPCORN . . . THE ONLY REASON YOU NEED TO STAY IN."

CARDAMOM AND CARAMEL
POPCORN (MAKES 8 CUPS)

Popcorn—you've gotta have it, so why not spice it up!

POPCORN
- 3 tablespoons peanut oil
- ⅓ cup popcorn kernels

CARDAMOM CARAMEL
- ½ cup (1 stick) unsalted butter
- 1 cup dark brown sugar
- ½ cup corn syrup
- 3 teaspoons ground cardamom

- 1 teaspoon salt
- 1 teaspoon vanilla extract
- ½ teaspoon baking soda

To make the popcorn, heat the oil in a saucepan over medium-high heat. Put 3 or 4 popcorn kernels into the oil and cover the pan. When the kernels pop, add the remaining kernels in an even layer. Leave the cover ajar to release steam. Gently shake the pan once the popping noise starts. Once the popping slows to several seconds between pops, remove the pan from the heat. Remove the lid and immediately pour the popcorn into a wide bowl.

To make the caramel, melt the butter in a saucepan over medium heat. Stir in the brown sugar, corn syrup, cardamom, and salt. Bring to a boil, stirring constantly. Let boil for 4 minutes. Remove from the heat and stir in the vanilla and baking soda. Pour in a thin stream over the popcorn, stirring to coat.

LOUKOU BEIGNETS (MAKES 24 BEIGNETS)

In Greek, λουκουμάδε—pronounced "loo-koo-MAH-thes"—are a staple in the Greek diet. These light deep-fried puffs drizzled with honey are a New Year's Eve tradition in many parts of Greece, and a sweet enjoyed at Hanukkah. So, as my mother is Greek and my father Jewish, I had to include these since they are part of our "Grewish" tradition twice a year.

- 2 cups fresh orange juice, strained to remove pulp
- 1 envelope or 2¼ teaspoons yeast
- 4½ cups all-purpose flour
- 1 teaspoon sugar
- 1 teaspoon salt
- 1 cup canola oil
- ½ cup orange blossom honey
- 2 tablespoons ground cinnamon

Warm 1 cup of the orange juice in the microwave, about 1 minute on low power. Add the yeast to the warm orange juice and stir to dissolve. In a large bowl, beat the orange juice–yeast mixture, 4 cups of the flour, and the sugar with an electric mixer until smooth. Cover and set aside in a warm place.

When the volume has doubled in size, about 30 minutes, add the remaining 1 cup orange juice, the remaining ½ cup flour, and the salt to make a thick batter. Cover again and allow the mixture to rise until it begins to bubble, about 1 hour.

Heat the oil in a deep skillet over medium heat. Line a metal tray with paper towels. When the oil begins to smoke, add the dough in level tablespoonfuls. Reduce the heat to medium-low and cook until the dough puffs and turns golden brown, about 2 minutes. Remove with a slotted spoon. Drain briefly on the paper towels. Transfer to a platter and pour honey over top. Sprinkle with cinnamon and serve hot.

POMEGRANATE
GRANITA (SERVES 8)

Granita . . . such a fancy word for shaved ice.

- **7 cups pure pomegranate juice**
- **1 cup fresh lemon juice**
- **1 tablespoon superfine sugar, or more to taste**
- **8 fresh mint leaves**

In a large bowl, combine the pomegranate juice, lemon juice, and sugar. Freeze until solid, about 5 hours.

To serve, use a spoon to scrape out large crystals and put into chilled glasses. Top with the mint leaves.

CARLA'S PUMPKIN TRIFLE (SERVES 8)

Mike Colletti's girlfriend—also known as Carla—is probably a better chef than he is! She comes to visit from New Jersey and in a day or two whips up the best Italian food we've ever eaten. She came over to my sister's house for a dinner and made this amazing trifle dessert. Car's birthday is on Halloween, so this was the perfect mix of pudding-to-cake-to-rum-soaked raisins (how can you go wrong with that!) for a fall treat. Of course, she had to include the pignoli, or pine nuts, to give it that Italian touch. The cake keeps well for several hours in the refrigerator.

PUDDING
- 1 16-ounce can pumpkin pie filling
- 1½ cups whole milk
  Half of a 7-ounce can sweetened condensed milk
- 1 5-ounce package instant vanilla pudding

SPICE CAKE
- 1¾ cups all-purpose flour, plus more for the pan
- 1⅓ cups dark brown sugar
- ½ cup whole milk
- ⅓ cup unsalted butter, plus more for the pan, softened
- 2 large eggs
- 3 teaspoons baking powder
- ½ teaspoon ground cinnamon
- ½ teaspoon ground nutmeg
- 1 cup dark rum
- 1 cup dark raisins
- 1 cup pine nuts

WHIPPED CREAM
- 1 cup chilled heavy cream
- ¼ cup confectioners' sugar
- 1 teaspoon vanilla extract
- 1 teaspoon ground cinnamon
- 1 teaspoon ground nutmeg
- ½ teaspoon ground cloves

Preheat the oven to 350°F. Butter and flour a 9-inch square baking dish.

To make the pudding, mix together the pumpkin pie filling, whole milk, sweetened condensed milk, and instant vanilla pudding in a large bowl and refrigerate, covered, for at least 1 hour, or until firm.

To make the cake, in a large bowl, beat together the flour, brown sugar, milk, butter, eggs, baking powder, cinnamon, and nutmeg with an electric mixer. Spoon into the prepared pan. Bake for 30 minutes, or until a knife inserted in the middle comes out clean. Remove from the oven and set the pan on a rack to cool.

Meanwhile, combine the rum and the raisins in a bowl, and let the raisins soak for 30 minutes. Preheat the broiler and spread the pine nuts out in a single layer on a baking sheet. Toast for 5 minutes, stirring to prevent burning.

To make the whipped cream, whip the cream with an upright mixer with the balloon whisk attachment or a handheld electric beater until almost stiff. Gradually add the sugar, beating until well mixed. Add the vanilla, cinnamon, nutmeg, and cloves, and beat until the cream holds peaks. Chill until ready to use.

When the cake is cool, drain the raisins and set aside. Break up the cake into pieces, and layer the pudding, whipped cream, and cake pieces evenly in a trifle bowl, arranging the layers so they are visible. Garnish with the pine nuts and raisins over top.

BIRTHDAY
CAKE (MAKES ONE 9-INCH CAKE)

Like we say at Good Stuff Eatery, every day is your birthday!

CAKE
- 1 cup (2 sticks) unsalted butter, plus more for the pan, softened
- 2 cups granulated sugar
- 4 large eggs, at room temperature
- 1½ cups self-rising flour
- 1¼ cups all-purpose flour
- 1 cup whole milk
- 1 teaspoon vanilla extract

CHOCOLATE ICING
- 5 cups confectioners' sugar
- ¾ cup unsweetened cocoa powder
- 6 tablespoons (¾ stick) unsalted butter
- ¾ cup evaporated milk
- 2 teaspoons vanilla extract

To make the cake, preheat oven to 350°F. Butter two 9-inch round cake pans.

In a large bowl, beat the butter with an electric mixer until smooth. Add the sugar gradually and beat until fluffy, about 3 minutes. Add the eggs, one at a time, beating well after each addition. Combine the flours and add in two parts, alternating with the milk and vanilla, beating well after each addition.

Divide batter among the cake pans. Bake for 20 to 25 minutes, or until a knife inserted into center of cake comes out clean. Remove from the oven and set the pans on a rack to cool for 10 minutes. Remove the cakes from the pans and cool completely on the rack.

Meanwhile, to make the icing, in a medium bowl, sift together the confectioners' sugar and cocoa and set aside. In a large bowl, beat the butter with an electric mixer until smooth. Gradually beat in the sugar mixture, alternating with the evaporated milk. Add the vanilla. Beat until light and fluffy. When cake layers have cooled, spread the icing on top of one layer, stack the other layer on top, then ice the top of the cake.

FAVORS 'N' FLAVORS:
PARTY DISHES

SPICY FIRE WINGS WITH SPICED APPLE CIDER
PEACH ICED TEA
TIGER TAIL
MARGARITA SLUSHIES
BLOODY MARY
HONEY-ROSEMARY LEMONADE
OPA! OUZO MARTINI
CINNAMON TWISTED DONUTS
BLACK RICE PUDDING WITH MANGO AND HAZELNUT

7

When whirling around a **cocktail** party or special event, everyone wants the perfect nibble, nosh, or nice, tall drink. Anything less than the best can be disastrous. (How miserable is a party where you leave starving?) Having been to a soiree or two in my life, I've thought of some **stellar recipes** that quench and satisfy without anyone feeling too stuffed, too sloshed, or too sticky. Party on!

SPICY FIRE WINGS WITH SPICED
APPLE CIDER (SERVES 12)

If you're feeling like a frugalista, this is a delish dish that doesn't cost much moolah but never feels anything less than indulgent. Wings have always been my foolproof way of wowing a crowd without getting all fancy and foie gras on 'em.

You can find the tamarind concentrate for the spicy glaze in a pint-size container at most Asian markets, and some grocery stores sell it in their international sections. The measures for the apple cider spices are just suggestions, as are the measures for the wings' spice mix—if you don't have any juniper berries or happen not to like coriander, omit them.

SPICED APPLE CIDER
- 1 gallon apple cider
- 3 cinnamon sticks
- 5 pieces star anise
- 2 whole cloves
- ½ cup juniper berries, optional
- 4 allspice berries

WINGS
- 2 cups packed dark brown sugar
- About ½ cup spice mix (about ¼ cup hot paprika, ¼ cup chili powder, 2 teaspoons ground coriander, 2 teaspoons five-spice powder, and 1 teaspoon ground cinnamon)
- 1 tablespoon ground cinnamon
- 10 pounds chicken wings

SPICY GLAZE
- ½ cup chopped assorted fresh chiles
- ½ cup hoisin sauce
- ½ cup tamarind liquid (see recipe introduction)
- 6 garlic cloves, crushed and chopped
- 3 shallots, sliced
- 1 tablespoon rice wine vinegar

To make the cider, heat the apple cider in a large saucepan over medium-low heat. Toast the spices, separated, in a large skillet over medium-low heat until they become fragrant. Stir to prevent scorching. Add each to the warm cider and set aside for the flavors to steep.

To make the wings, preheat the oven to 200°F. In a large bowl, combine the brown sugar, spice mix, and cinnamon and mix well. Add the wings to spice mix in batches and toss. Put on a baking sheet. Roast for 45 minutes.

Meanwhile, to make the glaze, heat a large skillet over medium heat and add the chiles, hoisin sauce, tamarind, garlic, shallots, and vinegar. Simmer for 30 minutes.

Preheat the grill or broiler. Brush the roasted wings with the glaze. Finish them on the grill or under the broiler, 2½ minutes on each side, to set the glaze. If you prefer a bit more burnt flavor, you can cook for a few minutes longer. Reheat the cider, strain out the whole spices, and serve it with the wings.

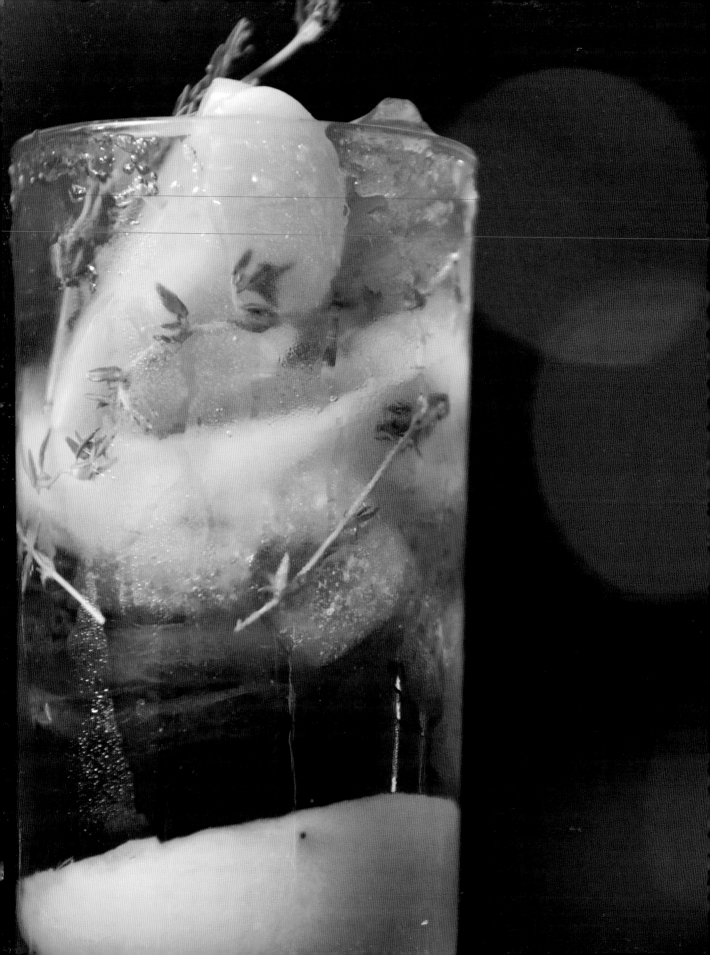

PEACH ICED TEA (SERVES 4)

I think we can all agree anything with peach schnapps is a par-tea!

- 6 peaches
- 4 cups cold water
- 4 tea bags jasmine tea, or 4 teaspoons loose leaves
- 4 ounces peach schnapps
- Juice from 1 lemon
- 1 lemon, sliced in circles, for garnish

Bring a large pot of water to a boil, add the peaches, and blanch for about 30 seconds. Remove the peaches and peel. Cut the peaches into eighths.

Bring the 4 cups water to a boil in a large saucepan. Steep the tea to your preferred strength. Add the peaches and schnapps to a blender and puree. When the tea is steeped, add the peach puree and lemon juice. Pour the peach tea into a large pitcher and chill. To serve, pour over ice cubes in four tall glasses and garnish with lemon slices.

TIGER TAIL (SERVES 4)

This was my favorite cocktail at Mai House, the Vietnamese restaurant I worked at in Tribeca, New York. It's an acquired hot, spicy taste but worth the risk. You can find ready-made passion fruit puree online, but it is also available at well-stocked Hispanic markets, where it may be sold as maracuya. You'll need 4 ounces of the puree for this recipe. Otherwise, find fresh passion fruit seasonally and follow the recipe below to make your own.

PASSION FRUIT PUREE
- 2 passion fruits
- ⅓ cup sugar

- 1 teaspoon fresh lime juice
- 6 ounces Absolut Peppar vodka

- 6 ounces triple sec
- 1 cup ice cubes
- 4 Thai chiles

To make the Passion Fruit Purée, cut the passion fruit open, scoop out the pulp, and add it to a blender. Add the sugar and puree. With the motor still running, add the lime juice (to prevent browning).

Add 1½ ounces of the vodka, 1½ ounces of the triple sec, 1 ounce of the passion fruit puree, and some of the ice to a martini shaker. Shake well. Strain into a chilled martini glass. Garnish with a chile. Repeat with the remaining ingredients.

MARGARITA SLUSHIES (SERVES 4)

It's funny that some people call me a food snob, when my favorite treat in life might seriously be a slushie. When I start making "real money" (movie star salary), I am so getting a slushie machine in my house.

- 8 cups water
- 12 ounces tequila
- 8 ounces triple sec
- 2 cup crushed ice

In batches of two servings at a time, or individually, add the water, tequila, triple sec, and crushed ice to a cocktail shaker. Shake well. Pour into glasses or chill in the freezer before serving.

BLOODY MARY (SERVES 4)

I'm not a big boozer, but even I can attest to the pure bliss otherwise known as a bloody Mary after a big night out. I prefer them with olives, my sister insists on fresh, crunchy celery, and Colletti tackles 'em with Tabasco sauce.

- 8 ounces vodka
- 16 ounces bloody Mary mix
- 2 teaspoons fresh lime juice
- 2 teaspoons prepared horseradish
- Pinch sea salt
- Pinch freshly ground black pepper
- 4 celery sticks, for garnish

Fill a tall, 8-ounce glass with ice. Add 2 ounces vodka, 4 ounces bloody Mary mix, $\frac{1}{2}$ teaspoon lime juice, and $\frac{1}{2}$ teaspoon horseradish. Stir well and garnish with salt, pepper, and celery stick. Repeat with the remaining ingredients.

"PURE BLISS AFTER
A BIG NIGHT OUT"

HONEY-ROSEMARY LEMONADE (SERVES 4)

One of the many highlights of living on Capitol Hill is the rosemary bush in front of my brown-stone. I'm never too beat to cut off some twigs and concoct a pitcher of honey-rosemary lemon-ade—sweet and thirst quenching.

 4 cups water, divided
1½ cups sugar
 2 sprigs fresh rosemary,
   plus more for garnish
 ½ cup honey
   Juice from 7 lemons
   Lemon slices, for garnish

Heat 1 cup of water, sugar, and 2 rosemary sprigs in a pot over medium heat and bring to a boil. Let boil for 7 minutes. Remove from the heat, cover, and let steep for 1½ hours.

Once cool, add the honey, lemon juice, and 3 cups of water (add additional water to taste). Remove the rosemary sprigs. Strain the lemonade into a pitcher and chill. Serve garnished with fresh rosemary sprigs and lemon slices.

OPA! OUZO MARTINI (SERVES 4)

The first time I tried ouzo, I drank an entire bottle like it was apple juice. Ouch. Since then, I've learned to ask for a little and sip it slowly. If you like black licorice or the best buzz under the sun, an ouzo martini will make your world a better place.

 6 ounces ouzo
 6 ounces vodka
 4 teaspoons fresh lemon
   juice
 4 cups ice cubes
 4 lemon slices, for garnish

Add 1½ ounces of the ouzo, 1½ ounces of the vodka, 1 teaspoon of the lemon juice, and 1 cup of the ice to a martini shaker. Shake well. Strain into a chilled martini glass. Garnish with a slice of lemon. Repeat with the remaining ingredients.

CINNAMON TWISTED DONUTS (MAKES 24)

My Southern pal summarizes these donuts quite eloquently: dangggg.

- 1 envelope or 2¼ teaspoons yeast
- 4½ cups all-purpose flour
- ½ cup plus 1 teaspoon sugar
- 1 teaspoon salt
- ⅓ cup ground cinnamon
- 1 cup canola oil

Warm 1 cup water in a large bowl in the microwave, about 2 minutes on high power. Add the yeast to the warm water and stir to dissolve. When the yeast starts to foam, add 4 cups of the flour and the ½ cup sugar and beat with an electric mixer until smooth. Cover and set aside in a warm place.

When the mixture's volume has doubled, after about 1 hour, add 1 cup of water, the salt, and the remaining ½ cup flour to make a thick batter. Cover again and allow the dough to rise until it begins to bubble, about 1½ hours.

In another bowl, combine the cinnamon and the 1 teaspoon sugar, mixing well.

Heat the oil in a deep skillet over medium heat until it smokes. Meanwhile, divide the dough into 24 uniform balls. Take 1 ball and roll it out into a 4-inch length. Put a finger in the center of the length and twist the dough around it to form a loop. Repeat with the remaining balls. Carefully lower a few twists at a time into the oil with a slotted spoon (do not crowd the skillet) and reduce the heat to medium-low. Fry until the puffs turn golden brown. Remove with a slotted spoon and drain on paper towels. Put on a tray. Sprinkle with the cinnamon sugar and serve hot.

BLACK RICE PUDDING WITH MANGO AND HAZELNUT (SERVES 4)

I can't say this is better than traditional rice pudding with a sprinkle of cinnamon—that's a classic—but it's different, delectable, and exotic. Mango, hazelnut, and black rice? Pretty interesting, right? It has a nice smooth flavor that's complemented by a sweet, nutty topping. You can find black rice at Asian or Middle Eastern specialty markets.

1 cup black rice, rinsed thoroughly

4 8-ounce cans coconut juice

2 cups sugar, plus more

1 8-ounce can coconut milk

1 mango, diced

½ cup crushed hazelnuts

To a large pot, add the rice, coconut juice, and sugar. Stir to combine and bring to a low boil over medium heat, about 20 minutes. When bubbles start to form, reduce the heat and cook until rice is softened, about 30 minutes more.

Add the coconut milk and taste. If it's not sweet enough, add a few tablespoons of sugar at a time until just right.

Distribute evenly among four bowls. Garnish with the mango and hazelnuts.